Economic Capital Modelling

Economic Capital Modelling
Concepts, Measurement and Implementation

Edited by
Iman van Lelyveld

Published by Risk Books, a Division of Incisive Financial Publishing Ltd

Haymarket House
28–29 Haymarket
London SW1Y 4RX
Tel: +44 (0)20 7484 9700
Fax: +44 (0)20 7484 9800
E-mail: books@incisivemedia.com
Sites: www.riskbooks.com
        www.incisivemedia.com

ISBN 1 904339 39 5

British Library Cataloguing in Publication Data
A catalogue record for this book is available from the British Library

Publisher: Laurie Donaldson
Development Editor: Steve Fairman
Designer: Rebecca Bramwell

Typeset by Mizpah Publishing Services Private Limited, Chennai, India

Printed and bound in Spain by Espacegrafic, Pamplona, Navarra

Contents

List of Contributors   vii

1 **Economic Capital: An Overview**   1
Maarten Gelderman, Pieter Klaassen, Iman van Leyveld

Introduction
The Importance of Risk Measurement
Approaches to Modelling Risk
Measures of Risk: Economic Capital
Regulatory Considerations
Concluding Remarks

2 **Risk Measurement within Financial Conglomerates:
Best Practices by Risk Type**   13
Klaas Knot, Jaap Bikker, Henk van Broekhoven,
Hugo Everts, Harry Horsmeier, Pieter Klaassen,
Iman van Lelyveld, Raymond Monnik, Francis Ruijgt,
Gaston Siegelaer, Henrico Wanders

Risk Typology
Market/ALM Risk
Credit and Transfer Risk
Life Risk
Non-Life or Property and Casualty Risk
Operational Risk
Business or Strategic Risk
Conclusion

3 **Appropriate Risk Measures, Time Horizon and
Valuation Principles in Economic Capital Models**   59
Gaston Siegelaer, Henrico Wanders

Introduction
Risks, Risk Measures and Economic Capital
One Risk Measure for All Stakeholders?
Experiences of Financial Conglomerates
Appropriate Time Horizons in Economic Capital
Valuation Principles
Concluding Remarks

4 **Diversification and Aggregation of Risks in Financial
Conglomerates**   79
Hugo Everts, Hartwig Liersch

Introduction
Correlation, Netting, Concentration and Granularity
Measurement Approaches

Aggregation Approaches
Estimation of Diversification Benefits
Allocation
Data Quality and Mis-Estimation
Regulatory Considerations

5 **A Survey of Economic Capital Model Implementation**   **113**
Iman van Lelyveld, Moncef Boughanmi,
Henk van Broekhoven, Hugo Everts,
Maarten Gelderman, Olav Jones, Pieter Klaassen,
Hartwig Liersch, Raymond Monnik, André Pouw,
Gaston Siegelaer, Henrico Wanders

Introduction
Previous Surveys
Objectives for Economic Capital Models
Implementation of Economic Capital Models: An Overview
General Remarks about All Risk Types
Approaches per Risk Type
Future Extensions
Concluding Remarks

6 **A Supervisory View on Economic Capital Models**   **137**
Iman van Lelyveld

Introduction
Regulatory Developments
Principles for Economic Capital Models
Supervisory Issues
Concluding Remarks

Annex A: Coherent and Insurance Risk Measures   **169**

**Annex B: Example of Violation of Sub-Additivity
Property of the VAR Measure**   **171**

List of Abbreviations   **173**

References   **175**

Index   **183**

List of Contributors

Jaap Bikker is a senior researcher at the strategy department, Supervisory Policy Division, De Nederlandsche Bank NV (DNB). His research interests are banking, insurance and pensions, financial conglomerates, risk management, competition and efficiency and procyclicality and regulation. He has published many articles in international money, banking and finance journals. Before joining the Supervisory Policy Division in 1997, Jaap was unit head of research at the European Monetary Institute (the predecessor of the European Central Bank (ECB)) in Frankfurt am Main and senior researcher at the research department of DNB. He held a position at the Free University in Amsterdam during 1977–1983 and, part-time, during 2003–2004. Jaap holds a master's degree and a PhD in econometrics from the Free University.

Moncef Boughanmi joined Rabobank in 1998. After having worked as a market risk manager for three years, he joined the economic capital project team in 2001, setting up an economic capital framework intended to be Basel II compliant. Moncef has recently moved to the economic capital analytics department within Rabobank Group Risk Management. He graduated in econometrics from the Université d'Aix-Marseille. He also holds a post graduate degree in econometrics (Diplome des Études Approfondies (DEA) in "Économie mathématique et économétrie").

Henk van Broekhoven began his career at the department for group business at Nationale Nederlanden, a Dutch insurer. After becoming an actuary, he started a research team within Nationale Nederlanden. Since 1990 he has been involved in the development of mortality tables for the Dutch market and later on also for the Dutch Actuarial Society (population tables). Since 1998, Henk has been with the ING group specialising in mortality issues, modelling economic capital and constructing models for diversification. He has worked on solvency issues for the International Actuarial

Association (IAA) in several working parties. Presently he is vice chair of the IAA solvency sub committee. Henk is involved in the development of Solvency II in an advisory capacity, chairing the working group "groups and conglomerates" and as a member of the project team.

Hugo Everts is head of capital allocation at ING Group Corporate Control and Finance in Amsterdam. In this function he is responsible for the risk-adjusted return on economic capital (RAROC) framework and quarterly reporting for the banking operations. Recently Hugo led the development for integrated – bank and insurance – risk measurement. He joined ING Asset and Liability Management in 1996 and later worked for Corporate Market Risk Management. Early career steps included positions at a specialised ship finance company and the Netherlands Bankers' Association. Hugo holds a master's degree in business economics from the Erasmus University of Rotterdam.

Maarten Gelderman studied business administration at Vrije Universiteit Amsterdam. In 1997 he obtained his PhD at this same institution. He has published nationally and internationally on accounting, finance, research methodology and information systems. In 2000 Maarten joined DNB's supervisory strategy department, which he headed from 2003 until the merger with the Dutch insurance and pension fund supervisor in 2004. Since then, he has been head of the joint supervisors' Quantitative Risk Management Department. This department is responsible for the design and implementation of risk-based solvency regimes for banks (Basel II), insurers (Solvency II), pension funds (Financial Assessment Framework) and financial conglomerates. Maarten chaired the Working Group on Economic Capital Models, which consisted of experts from the industry and the supervisory agencies. He also chairs the Basel Committee's Accord Implementation Validation Subgroup and is a member of various other international groups.

Harry Horsmeier is market manager of Towers Perrin–Tillinghast in the Netherlands. In this capacity, he is responsible for Towers Perrin–Tillinghast business in the Benelux. Prior to this he worked for Fortis for over 20 years. His last position within Fortis was that of group actuary. Harry holds a master's degree in actuarial science from the Free University. He is a full member of the Actuarieel Genootschap, the Dutch actuarial association, and an honorary member of the Institute of Actuaries in England.

Olav Jones joined Fortis in 2002 as head of Insurance Risk. He has over 14 years of experience working in the fields of risk, capital and value-based management within large financial organisations. Before joining Fortis, he started his career with Oliver, Wyman & Co and then worked for Prudential Plc. Within Fortis Olav focuses specifically on insurance risk. He has a co-ordination role for projects relating to embedded value reporting, provision adequacy and economic capital across all insurance businesses within the Fortis Group and for strategic risk issues such as Solvency II. Currently Olav is chairman of the Comité Européen des Assurances (CEA) Solvency II Steering Group. He has a degree in engineering from Exeter University and a masters in finance from Cambridge University.

Pieter Klaassen is senior vice-president of Enterprise Risk Modelling within Group Risk Management of ABN AMRO Bank. In this capacity, he is responsible for the development of quantitative models to measure the integrated risk profile of the bank and its business units, comprising all major risk types (credit, market, country, operational, business and asset liability management (ALM) risks). These models perform a central role in the bank's risk and portfolio management activities, capital allocation and performance management. Before joining ABN AMRO Bank in 1998, he worked at Rabobank International in Utrecht. He also had a part-time research position at the Free University in Amsterdam until 2004. Pieter holds a master's degree in econometrics from Erasmus University Rotterdam, and a PhD degree in operations research from Massachusetts Institute of Technology.

Klaas Knot is currently division director of Supervisory Policy at DNB, where he is responsible for the development of prudential standards and instruments for banks, insurers, pension funds and investment firms. He was previously associated with the International Monetary Fund and the Dutch Pensions and Insurance Supervisory Authority (PVK). Klaas is also a part-time professor of money and banking at the University of Groningen. He has published many articles in leading (international) professional journals in the field of monetary and financial economics.

Iman van Lelyveld is policy advisor at DNB, active in the development of the Supervisory Review, risk management and banking research. He is a member of the Research Task Force (RTF), which reports to the Basel Committee and which coordinates research efforts among member institutions. Presently he is chair of a RTF group working on stress testing. In addition, Iman holds a part-time associate professorship at Radboud University, teaching amongst others international financial management and banking. He has published work on financial conglomerates, interbank contagion and foreign banking in Central and Eastern Europe. He studied macroeconomics at the University of Amsterdam and a PhD in applied economics from Radboud University. He started his career at Deutsche Bank.

Hartwig Liersch is principal of Capital Allocation at Internationale Nederlanden Group (ING) Group Corporate Control and Finance in Amsterdam, the Netherlands. He is responsible for development and reporting of ING bank's economic capitals that are at the basis of the bank's key performance indicator, the risk-adjusted return on capital (RAROC). Hartwig is also involved in recent projects linked to the introduction of integrated risk management at ING group level. Previously, he worked within asset and liability management, the Netherlands and the research department of ING Bank Controlling. He holds a master's degree in economics/econometrics from the University of Münster, Germany.

Raymond Monnik graduated in 1988 with a BA in international management from the Hogere Economische School Amsterdam. In 2000 he received his MBA from the University of Rochester (USA) and Nyenrode University (the Netherlands). After a traineeship at ABN AMRO, from 1990 to 1994, he held various positions at ING Bank, ranging from Eurobond trader to syndication manager of Equity Capital Markets. From 1994 to 1996 Raymond worked at ING Barings in London as assistant director of Equity Capital Markets. In 1996 he continued his career at Rabobank. Starting off as a relationship manager for Financial Institutions, he became a member of the management team of the Group Treasury in 1997. In the treasury department he was responsible for the management of credit risk resulting from trading activities. From 2000 to 2005 he was project manager for economic capital, also responsible for the implementation of a BIS II compliant economic capital framework in Rabobank Group. Since July 2005, Raymond has been within Credit Portfolio Management at Rabobank Nederland.

André Pouw has extensive practical experience in accounting and financial reporting. He has been with Fortis since 1968 as a controller of insurance, finance/banking, investment and property development companies. For a number of years he has been responsible for the back office of a Fortis asset manager, active as compliance officer and involved in risk management. Since 2003, he has been an (internal) advisor on accounting issues, especially related to IFRS and Solvency II. André has represented Fortis in accounting forums of national and international bodies (eg, VNO/NCW (Confederation of Netherlands Industry and Employers); Verbond van Verzekeraars (Dutch Association of Insurers); CFO Forum). He has several accounting degrees from basic accounting through to the level of auditor (Dutch chartered accountant).

Francis Ruijgt joined Nationale Nederlanden (NN) in 1974, moving to ING Group's Corporate Insurance Risk Management as deputy chief insurance risk officer in 1995. Over time, his responsibilities have included technical support in asset and liability risk management, accounting, reserve adequacy and developing standards applicable to all business units and business lines. In 1999 he initiated the development of an economic capital model for ING's insurance business. Most recently his focus has been on external developments in accounting and solvency. Francis is heavily involved in international industry organisations, particularly in the area of accounting and solvency. These involvements include: co-vice-chair of the IAA (International Actuarial Association) committee on Insurance Accounting Standards, co-chair of the IAA Subcommittee on Actuarial Standards and Member of the IASB Financial Instruments Working Group. Francis holds a master's degree in econometrics from the

University of Tilburg and is a fellow of the Actuarieel Genootschap, the Dutch actuarial society.

Gaston Siegelaer studied econometrics at Tilburg University, the Netherlands. In 1990 he started working with Robeco Group in Rotterdam. He specialised in asset liability modelling and quantitative investment research. In June 1996 he obtained his PhD from the Erasmus University Rotterdam for his thesis on strategic investment and funding policy for pension funds. In late 1996 he joined the Pensions and Insurance Supervisory Authority of the Netherlands, where he was involved in research and policy advice on the issues of investment, risk management and solvency. From February 2000 until December 2002 Gaston was head of research. From 2002 until 2004 he was project manager of the Financial Assessment Framework. He is currently working as a senior policy advisor within the Supervisory Policy division of DNB. Since early 2005 he has specialised in securitisation regulation. He was a member of working parties of the Dutch Actuarial Society on reinsurance and securitisation, and on economic scenarios.

Henrico Wanders is an actuarial analyst within the Actuarial Department of Univé Verzekeringen, a property and casualty insurer. He is implementing new risk management, especially the development of an economic capital model. From 2001 until 2006, he worked at the Pensioen- & Verzekeringskamer (Pensions and insurance supervisory authority of the Netherlands), and after the merging at De Nederlandsche Bank in the supervisory development division. In this position he was one of the members of the QIS-task force of the Financial Stability Committee of Ceiops. He also provided several contributions on the Financial Assessment Framework (FTK), especially with respect to the possible quantitative effects for life insurers and pension funds of a regime shift in the solvency regulation, and the reporting framework for pension funds. Henrico holds a master's degree in both econometrics and economics from the University of Groningen, and a PhD degree in management and organisation from the University of Groningen.

The authors support War Child Netherlands. War Child Netherlands is a Dutch non-profit organisation and is part of a network of independent organisations working across the world to support children affected by armed conflicts. War Child Netherlands specialises in providing psycho-social assistance to children in former war zones, using all kinds of creative methods. War Child Netherlands has its headquarters in Amsterdam, with projects in Africa, The Balkans, The Caucasus, Asia, and Latin-America. Royalties generated from this book will be donated to the projects of War Child Netherlands.

For more information: www.warchild.com

Economic Capital: An Overview

Maarten Gelderman, Pieter Klaassen, Iman van Leyveld

INTRODUCTION

This book covers all aspects of economic capital for financial conglomerates, ie, financial institutions that are active in both the banking and the insurance sector. Moreover, given the increasing convergence of risk measurement and management practices in both sectors, it should be of equal interest to either sector separately. One aspect that sets this book apart from any other book in this field is that it provides a balanced overview of economic capital; both from the perspective of (risk) managers within institutions and from a supervisor's point of view. In addition, it brings together both practitioners – risk managers and policymakers – and academics. Combining these insights in a single volume will contribute to an increasingly (mutual) understanding. Furthermore, the practitioners' view is not the view of a single institution, consultant or vendor but reflects the combined insights of a number of institutions that have cutting edge economic capital frameworks. Taken together, we feel that we have produced a book without comparison.

The first steps towards this book were taken in 2001 when Oliver, Wyman & Co delivered a report on the risk profile and capital adequacy of mixed financial conglomerates.[1] The report concluded that: (1) adding up stand-alone capital measures would not dramatically overstate capital at the holding company level, and that (2) internal capital frameworks would offer the best solutions to overcome limitations of what was dubbed the "silo approach". Accordingly, the primary role of the supervisor would be to review the internal risk assessment and the resulting capital allocation within financial conglomerates.

It was felt, however, that the Oliver, Wyman & Co report provided a valuable outline but also raised new questions, especially about the operation of economic capital models in practice. In order to get a deeper understanding of developments in this area the Working group on Economic Capital Models (WECM) was established, consisting of representatives of the Council of Financial Supervisors (Raad van Financiële Toezichthouders), the Dutch Banking Association (Nederlandse Vereniging van Banken), and the Dutch Insurance Association (Het Verbond). The objective of the working group is to conduct further research into internal economic capital models of bank and insurance activities, in order to assess their suitability to chart a financial conglomerate's risk profile.

To ensure balanced input from all stakeholders, the WECM was staffed with members from the Dutch financial industry and from the Dutch prudential regulator. Some participants in the group maintain close links with academia; all share day-to-day responsibility for their institutions internal models (in case of industry members) and the development of new supervisory approaches. Thus, this book goes beyond a pure academic exercise and recognises that economic capital is a relatively new and rapidly developing concept. Divergent views on best industry practice, and the fact that implementation may in practice be constrained by a lack of data, and the existence of legacy systems result in an amalgam that in the end is an institution's (or for that matter a regulator's) risk measurement system. The group hopes that this book helps the reader to get familiar with the relevant concepts, the way models are implemented in practice and the approach supervisors take with respect to internal models.

The WECM has periodically published papers and a compilation of these papers was presented at a conference organised by De Nederlandsche Bank on 12th May 2005. The title of the conference was "Integrated Supervision of Financial Conglomerates: Challenges for the Future". In the bundled papers, the WECM surveyed the state of the art of economic capital methodology. The specific aim was to investigate the commonalities and differences between the approaches used in banking and insurance companies, and how they are or can be integrated for financial conglomerates.

The present book is based on these working papers. New material was added in areas where, due to space constraints in the earlier working papers, subjects had only been covered in a broad-brush style. In addition, we took pains to remove any repetitive material.

The WECM has been a very fruitful platform for discussing such a rapidly developing subject as economic capital has turned out to be. This discussion would not have been possible without the contributions of all the members, past and present. The following persons have been active in the Working Group (in alphabetic order): J. Bikker (DNB), M. Boughanmi (RABO), H. van Broekhoven (ING), H. Everts (ING; former secretary), M. Gelderman (DNB; chair), H. Horsmeier (Fortis), O. Jones (Fortis), P. Klaassen (ABN AMRO), K. Knot (DNB; former chair), I. van Lelyveld (DNB, Radboud University), H. Liersch (ING; secretary), R. Monnik (RABO), A. Pouw (Fortis), F. Ruijgt (ING), G. Siegelaer (DNB) and H. Wanders (DNB).[2] Background information on each of the authors can be found in the biographies included above.

As a guide for the reader we will first provide an executive summary in the remainder of this first, introductory chapter. The first issue that we will cover is the importance of risk measurement. This discussion will lead us to two important questions: (1) how to discern risk types, and (2) how do we come an economic capital outcome once we have defined and measured risks? After providing answers to these questions to the best of our ability we turn to an extensive survey in to the present state of play at a number of large internationally active financial institutions. Finally, we present the supervisory view: what can or should a supervisor do with these economic capital models.

THE IMPORTANCE OF RISK MEASUREMENT

Calculated risk taking is at the heart of what financial companies in banking and insurance do. To a large extent, financial companies make their business out of pooling and transferring risk and the transformation of risks from one form into another. Consequently, risk measurement and risk management are as important to the financial sector as activities such as supply chain management and logistics are in more traditional undertakings.

Financial companies use risk measurement for a multitude of purposes. Adequate risk measurement will help companies to take up only those risks for which they will earn a decent return, for example, by reducing their exposure to idiosyncratic risk. It helps them to improve the risk/return relationship, by taking up those positions that best match their risk profile. Moreover, adequate risk measurement helps to deal with the potential (agency) problems that exist between different stakeholders in financial companies. A lack of inherent goal congruence between shareholders, supervisors, management and society at large (including individual customers) can be compensated for by means of risk-based contracts: supervisors (on behalf of society) require institutions to hold a, risk-based, minimum amount of risk-bearing capital (equity); shareholders want to ensure that managers run their institutions in such a way that they maximise the value of the undertaking as a whole, rather than "gambling the bank" in order to maximise their own return without being subject to possibly adverse scenarios. Within institutions, similar considerations apply. Despite the various stakeholders and their different objectives, economic capital has taken hold as a central risk measure that is relevant for all.

Against this background, numerous approaches to risk measurement have been developed both by academia, practitioners and supervisors.[3] Over the years, these approaches have simultaneously become increasingly risk sensitive and increasingly advanced (if not complicated). At the same time, this multitude of approaches, thanks to increased risk sensitivity, has become more similar. Although on the outside, models for different risk types, models from different industries and models developed by supervisors and the industry itself may seem to be worlds apart, beneath the surface these models take a rather comparable approach to risk measurement. Right now, we seem to be at a crossroads, where the industry's internal models and supervisory measures of required capital are speedily integrating. Basel II and Solvency II, although to different degrees and with material differences between different risk types, increasingly rely on internal models for setting regulatory required capital. Internally, institutions are increasingly taking an integrated approach to risk measurement and the acronyms of measures such as Return on Risk Adjusted Capital (RORAC) have become household names.

APPROACHES TO MODELLING RISK

In principle, two approaches to risk modelling are available: one can either start modelling an institution as a whole and next disaggregate outcomes (the top-down approach) or start at the bottom and work upwards (the bottom-up approach). A limitation of the top-down approach is that it does not clearly indicate how to manage and control the outcomes of the model. Consequently, bottom-up approaches tend to be more prevalent in practice. Underlying their application, however, are two major problem areas: (1) how to "divide" the calculations, and (2) how to aggregate the outcomes of the individual models. We will turn to each of these questions in the next two sub-sections.

Risk types

The first question amounts to specifying for which risk types models will be developed. Admittedly, any classification of risk types is somewhat arbitrary. Typically a classification will be driven by two considerations: (1) homogeneity; it makes more sense to combine similar risks, and (2) practicality; it is convenient when the classification matches the distribution of activities and responsibilities already prevalent in an organisation. After an investigation of existing classifications and real world practices within the participating institutions, the Working Group arrived at a classification that consists of the following risk types: (1) market/ALM, (2) credit, (3) life, (4) property and casualty (P&C) or non-life, (5) operational and (6) business or strategic. In Chapter 2 we will define the types in depth and discuss alternative typologies.

Risk drivers and aggregation: diversification effects

A crucial factor in the determination of the aggregate risk profile of an institution is the recognition of diversification effects. Since risks typically are not perfectly correlated, the aggregate risk of a financial company as a whole will be smaller than the sum of all the individual risks.

The diversification effect within a financial conglomerate largely depends on the specific correlation values of all acknowledged risk drivers. Interest rates as a risk driver, for instance, will not only affect market risk; but also, although to a more limited extent, credit risk (an increase in interest rates may lead to more defaults) and business risk (changing interest rates may make certain products and strategies more or less attractive). From a theoretical point of view, a system of risk aggregation that takes into account how sensitive the recognised risk types are to the various risk drivers seems preferable. However, in practice it is more realistic to determine the sensitivity to risk drivers within each risk type. Then, based on this information, correlations between risk types can be used to calculate an aggregate outcome.

We find that it is not worthwhile to determine a typical diversification benefit for an institution combining banking and insurance. Rather than being constant, the diversification benefit would depend on the sensitivity to individual risk drivers and consequently vary with the insurance and banking leg outcomes on the six risk types. This is easily seen by imagining a situation where the insurance leg transfers credit risk to the banking leg; this would not affect the risk profile of the group as a whole. Using a constant diversification effect between the bank and insurance leg, however, the estimate of group wide risk would depend on the distribution of credit risk over the banking and insurance leg. Such anomalies can be avoided by aggregating by risk type rather than industry. Although it is likely that an economic capital number is calculated for both the banking and the insurance leg, the aggregate capital number for the institution as a whole is not calculated by combining these two numbers, but by combining the underlying capital numbers for the individual risk types.

Although diversification benefits within a conglomerate depend on the actual situation of the institution there are clear areas where considerable risk reduction can be realised. Especially in the market risk/ALM area, the combination of bank and insurance may potentially lead to substantial exposure offsets (or "netting" effects) that occur when opposite sensitivities to the same risk driver (here: interest rates) are present.[4] Moreover, this benefit takes the form of a natural hedge and consequently is not subject to the problems associated with diversification effects that depend on an adequate estimate of correlation coefficients. Other clear benefits could come from diversifying the systematic risk of different businesses or strategies. Most promising candidates for diversification benefits between risk types are, for example, operational and non-life risk. Since we do not know the direct relation of the risk types with the more fundamental risk drivers, caution should be exercised when recognising this kind of diversification effects. More details on the relevant considerations for this subject can be found in Chapter 4.

MEASURES OF RISK: ECONOMIC CAPITAL

Given the choices in the definition of risk types, risk measures, time horizons etc it will become clear in Chapter 3 that a common pattern underlying all state-of-the-art models is that they ultimately determine a number called the economic capital. This number reflects the extent to which, at the company's desired level of comfort, in a given period results for (part of) an undertaking can be worse than originally expected, ie, it reflects unexpected losses (ULs). We argue that such losses should be determined using economic value (be it mark-to-market or mark-to-model). Even acknowledging that a certain amount of uncertainty is associated with marking to model, the usage of accrual values will almost certainly result in a larger misspecification of capital.

To the extent that supervisors rely on models, they tend to set a confidence level and a time horizon – often referred to as the holding period – and next require institutions to hold sufficient risk absorbing means (such as equity) to withstand a loss equal to the capital number determined. Since this number is defined by the supervisor, we refer to it as regulatory capital. Internally, institutions tend to follow similar approaches in calculating a capital amount (in this case typically referred to as internal or economic capital). In other words, they set a confidence level and time horizon and next determine the capital number. In this case, the outcome, however, tends to differ from capital held, but may be the number used in RORAC calculations and/or a capital level the institution is aiming for.

The way in which the capital number is determined, shows considerable variation. On the one extreme, the effects of one or more adverse scenarios are evaluated and the outcome is used as a capital number. A time horizon and confidence interval are only implicitly associated with this scenario. In the other extreme, a fully analytical approach is taken and a stylised model is used to calculate capital. In between are approaches such as historical and Monte Carlo simulation, where a data-based approach is taken to determine a distribution of potential losses over the time horizon. This distribution is then used to determine capital. Multiple approaches may be used simultaneously; institutions may for instance combine an analytical approach with a set of very severe scenarios in order to test the robustness of the outcomes.

The choice of which confidence level and holding period are employed depends on numerous circumstances. For the participating institutions, numbers above 99.95% are typical and tend to be determined by the external rating an institution is aiming for. The time horizon tends to be one year. Efficiency considerations and legacy systems may lead to deviations, however. An example is the treatment of market risk in banking, where some institutions use the supervisory model (with the 10-day holding period a 99% confidence level) and next scale the number in order to be consistent with their general risk measurement system.

The form and sophistication of internal models differs within and between institutions. Apart from the size of institutions (which was not relevant among industry representatives in the Working Group, who all are employed by large financial institutions), data availability, the availability of a common view on best industry practice play their respective roles. Market and ALM risk clearly benefit from the fact that an ample amount of high-frequency data is available. When modelling credit and insurance risks, data availability may easily become a constraint. For other risk types, the construction of accurate, detailed and consistent data sets remains a challenge.

Apart from size, data availability and the availability of best industry practice, external factors, and especially supervisory regulation, affect approaches taken by institutions. The example given about market risk is a point in case, but examples with a more positive flavour can be given as well. Among the industry representatives in the Working Group there is general agreement that the forthcoming introduction of Basel II created buy-in and speed, and thus gave an additional impulse to risk measurement in the banking area. Especially for credit risk and operational risk the form of the models used tends to be based on the same principles as the Basel II regulations. Thus, Basel II, by codifying best industry practice, reinforced a trend towards more convergence in risk management practices in banking. Moreover, Basel II led to industry wide initiatives

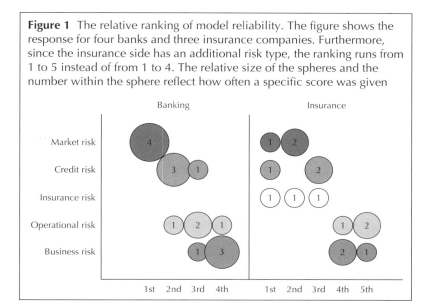

Figure 1 The relative ranking of model reliability. The figure shows the response for four banks and three insurance companies. Furthermore, since the insurance side has an additional risk type, the ranking runs from 1 to 5 instead of from 1 to 4. The relative size of the spheres and the number within the sphere reflect how often a specific score was given

for the collection of operational risk data, which may well have been crucial for the development of models in this area. In insurance, the risk-based regulation of the UK Financial Services Authority (FSA), the Dutch Financial Assessment Framework and the Swiss Solvency test are reinforcing a similar trend.

All this results in a situation depicted in Figure 1. Participants in the group consider market and ALM risk to be estimated most reliably. Credit risk comes a good second. More details on practices and the way different risk categories are approached by the institutions participating in the Working Group can be found in Chapter 5.

REGULATORY CONSIDERATIONS
Given the improvements institutions are making, it is understandable that arguments are made for full recognition of internal models in determining regulatory capital. When fully adopted such an approach would imply that internal and regulatory capital became identical or, alternatively, that regulatory capital would be determined using the same model as internal capital, but using a lower,

regulatory solvency standard. As indicated in the introduction of this document, supervisors are moving in this direction, but as yet, full models for an institution as a whole have not been allowed. Instead, supervisors take a piecemeal approach, accepting full models for individual risk categories (market risk and operational risk under Basel II) or allowing partial models only (credit risk under Basel II). Alternatively, internal models may be combined with a mechanically determined floor, in order to give supervisors a sufficient level of comfort; it is fairly likely that Solvency II will evolve in this direction. For purposes of supervisory review a tendency to increasingly rely on economic capital models is visible as well. General agreement seems to exist that, in order to allow for a move in this direction, models should be truly internal and should not be developed for regulatory purposes only. Supervisors are only willing to accept models when these remain internal, as may for instance be illustrated by the extent to which they are embedded in the organisation and are used for internal purposes such as pricing and performance related pay. That said; supervisors have to be attentive to a number of additional issues. The most important of these are the effects of recognising economic capital model use on competitive equality, the behaviour of the models in times of stress and, finally, the home-host aspect of model and model outcome recognition. These and other issues are discussed in more detail in Chapter 6.

CONCLUDING REMARKS
Over the last couple of years, risk measurement has undergone tremendous progress. This development is self re-enforcing. Institutions that gain more experience in risk measurement in a certain area tend to apply this experience to new domains and in new parts of their organisation. Increased reliance on economic capital models also stimulates data collection, which in turn helps to further refine the models.

A natural sequel to such developments is the employment of economic capital for supervisory purposes. Using the same models both internally and for regulatory purposes brings efficiency gains. Indeed, supervisors are moving in the direction of increased reliance on internal models. This implies a change where supervision increasingly comes in line with economic reality, rather than using fixed and less risk-sensitive rules. That said; supervisors require a level of comfort with overall capital levels. Models that are useful internally are as yet not always satisfactory for supervisory purposes. Over the next couple of years, however, we expect to see ever-increasing reliance on economic capital models. A first important milestone will be the implementation of Solvency II where internal models may well play a very prominent role. In the longer run, further revisions to the Basel framework may move this regime in a direction that is ever more oriented towards full internal modelling. Since internal models are based on economic reality rather than on inflexible rules, increased reliance on internal models will in the end also help to overcome inconsistencies in the regulatory solvency treatment of insurance and banking.

Authors of this chapter:
Maarten Gelderman, DNB; Pieter Klaassen, ABN AMRO and Iman van Leyveld, DNB.

1   See OWC (2001). Oliver, Wyman & Company changed its name in to Mercer Oliver Wyman in 2003.
2   Currently, Horsmeier is with Tillinghast Towers-Perrin and Wanders is with Univé.
3   Several books have appeared in recent years capturing this development (see, eg, Dev 2004; Bessis 2002; Matten 2001).
4   In order for this benefit to occur, it is of course assumed that this risk has not already been hedged away within one of the legs of the institution. Furthermore, the Working Group observes that benefits such as this are most likely to be realised with a central risk management function.

2

Risk Measurement within Financial Conglomerates: Best Practices by Risk Type

Klaas Knot, Jaap Bikker, Henk van Broekhoven, Hugo Everts, Harry Horsmeier, Pieter Klaassen, Iman van Lelyveld, Raymond Monnik, Francis Ruijgt, Gaston Siegelaer, Henrico Wanders

Economic capital models have recently come into vogue as a tool to measure risk and return on a firm-wide basis and to allocate capital accordingly. A prerequisite for a proper implementation of such models is a common language. This chapter aims to achieve a common risk language for the various stakeholders, each having their specific background. In practice, risk assessment and economic capital allocation still differs across banking and insurance activities, reflecting differences in the dominant risk types that have traditionally been discerned in each of the sectors. Banking institutions mainly focus on credit risk (with only more recent attention for additional risks such as market, interest rate and operational risk). On the other hand, insurance companies mainly focus on insurance-technical risks and ALM risk. In order to construct a common risk language across a financial conglomerate, the differences in the sector specific frameworks should be identified and, as much as possible, agreement should be sought on a joint framework that encompasses all relevant risks in a uniform way.

The chapter is organised as follows. First we will briefly define some key concepts in risk measurement and capital allocation. This will provide the background for the subsequent discussion of the risk types. More in-depth discussions will follow in later chapters. Then we present a table (Table 2) containing a classification of risk types that financial conglomerates typically distinguish. Each risk type will then in turn be elaborated upon in a separate section, presenting definitions, the main risk drivers and the various alternative approaches to quantify the risk.

Risk measurement and economic capital[1]

Financial institutions make a return by taking financial risks for their own account, or by accepting financial risks from customers. Institutions also generate income by providing services that aim to mitigate clients' risks. Within financial institutions, risks from individual clients – stemming from their inability to effectively deal with the frequency, timing and/or severity of contingent events themselves – will be transferred to a pool of similar risks.[2] Risk management can thus be seen as one of the core activities of a financial institution. In order to perform this activity in a controlled and well-informed manner, risk identification followed by risk measurement is a natural starting point. In the debate, risk measurement, risk assessment and risk management are often used interchangeably. In this chapter, risk measurement refers to the quantification of risk. Risk assessment is a broader concept in the sense that it also entails interpreting non-quantitative pieces of information. Risk management, in turn, encompasses risk assessment as well as risk mitigation.

Risk measurement – a generic term describing a wide variety of techniques – typically starts rather autonomously in the different business lines within a financial institution. To compare these techniques, however, one has to come up with an overall standard to measure risk. Recent developments within the financial industry have converged toward the use of economic capital as this common risk standard.

The exact definition of the economic capital concept differs across institutions however. In a recent survey of large, internationally active insurers (Societies of Actuaries 2004) the following alternative definitions were given (see Table 1).

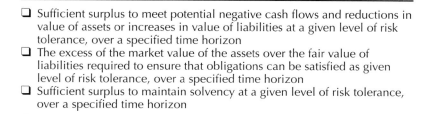

Table 1 Alternative definitions of economic capital

❏ Sufficient surplus to meet potential negative cash flows and reductions in value of assets or increases in value of liabilities at a given level of risk tolerance, over a specified time horizon
❏ The excess of the market value of the assets over the fair value of liabilities required to ensure that obligations can be satisfied as given level of risk tolerance, over a specified time horizon
❏ Sufficient surplus to maintain solvency at a given level of risk tolerance, over a specified time horizon

Source: (Societies of Actuaries 2004, Table 4.1, p 6). Based on 77 responses.

The first and the last of these alternative definitions mention "sufficient surplus" while the middle definition focuses on the determinants of the surplus (ie, the market value of the assets and the fair value of the liabilities). In particular, insurance companies that are part of a mixed conglomerate tend to use earnings-oriented approaches for calculating economic capital.

In the discussion of the Working Group, we arrived at a slightly different definition:

"Economic capital can be defined as the amount of capital that a transaction or business unit requires in order to support the economic risk it originates, as perceived by the institution itself."

This definition is in line with the second definition mentioned in Table 1. We highlight, however, two additional aspects that need to be mentioned. The first aspect is that ownership of the economic capital process lies with the institution. It is thus not something that is prescribed by outside parties such as rating agencies or supervisors. The second aspect is that one of the goals of economic capital modelling is to be able to allocate economic capital to business lines or activities. Such a risk measure can then also be used for risk-adjusted performance measurement, which compares returns to the risk incurred in earning those returns (such as RAROC and RORAC).

THE HISTORY OF RISK MEASUREMENT AND MANAGEMENT
Risk was first seriously studied during the Renaissance. The theory of probability first formulated by Blaise Pascal and Pierre de Fermat still lies at the heart of most modern risk measurement. Given the limited

space in the present book and the excellent account provided by Peter Bernstein in *"Against the Gods"* (Bernstein 1996), we will focus on the developments in recent history directly related to measuring and managing risks on a holistic basis in a large financial institution. These developments are presented graphically in Figure 2.

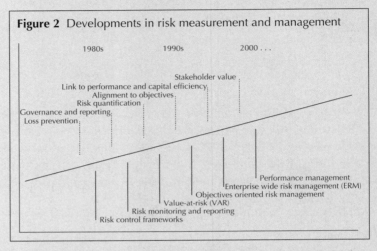

Figure 2 Developments in risk measurement and management

Focusing on the measurement of economic capital, we roughly see a development moving from concepts such as return on equity to return on capital to, finally, risk-adjusted return on capital. Return on equity (ROE) is the ratio of a given measure of earnings to own funds as they appear on the balance sheet. More precisely

$$ROE = \frac{Earnings}{Accounting\ own\ funds}$$

ROE does provide a measure of the overall performance of an institution but it is inadequate in analysing an institution's risk performance. In the management of risk, ROE has two major drawbacks. First, as the denominator is not risk sensitive ROE is an inadequate indicator. Second, and more importantly, ROE is generally only defined at the level of the institution as a whole as accounting own funds are not allocated to specific business lines. This invalidates ROE as an instrument to manage risks across business lines.

To improve risk management, the accounting own funds in the ROE equation have been replaced by capital allocated to specific business lines. This is called return on capital (ROC) and is given by

$$ROC_i = \frac{Earnings_i}{Capital\ charge_i}$$

The numerator in the latter formula is the same as in the first equation defining the ROE. The exact definition of earnings and the precise method of allocating economic capital across business lines differ across institutions. ROC is a better measure of profitability but still does not take in to account the variability or risk of the earnings. To this end both the numerator and the denominator of the ROE equation are adjusted for risk, yielding RAROC.[3] It is generally defined in the following way (cf, Matten 2001):

$$RAROC = \frac{Profit}{Risk\text{-}adjusted\ capital} = \frac{\begin{array}{l} Revenues \\ -expenses \\ -expected\ losses \\ +\ return\ on\ economic\ capital \\ \pm\ transfer\ values/prices \end{array}}{\begin{array}{l} Capital \\ Capital\ reserved\ to\ cover\ worst\text{-}case\ loss\ (minus\ expected\ losses) \\ to\ required\ confidence\ threshold \\ (eg,\ 99\%)\ for\ relevant\ risks \end{array}}$$

Risk adjusted or economic capital is used in measuring, monitoring and managing risks. RAROC is used for assessing and optimising risk adjusted returns and is used to allocate capital across business lines. It is thus helpful in improving comprehensive risk management.

Risk is a concept that is given different definitions, depending on the context; an often-applied definition in the context of capital management is unexpected loss or "UL".[4] Risk is a function of the volatility of outcomes – the expected outcome can be compared with the mean of all possible outcomes, and risk relates to the variability of outcomes. Economic capital can then be defined in more operational terms as a buffer against all ULs, including those not incurred on the balance sheet (such as potential loss arising from a derivatives position or a guarantee), at the company's desired level of comfort. The statistical analysis essentially ascertains the potential maximum loss in value of assets and other exposures (or increase in value of liabilities) over a given time period, at a given confidence interval.

The concept of UL relates to the loss in market value, not in accounting earnings. This concept is also reflected in VAR, a statistical technique that is often applied for measuring market risk in banking (see the "Market risk" section in Chapter 2). Figure 3 shows the workings of the VAR technique graphically. The curve represents

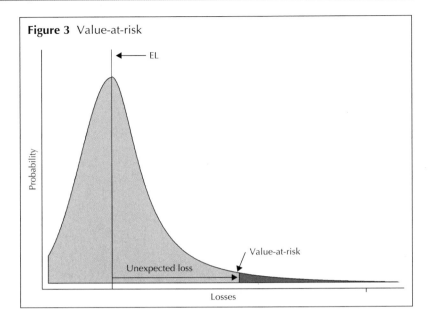

Figure 3 Value-at-risk

the distribution of losses for a fictitious portfolio. The shape of this loss distribution depends on the portfolio in question. The darkly shaded area corresponds with a certain, pre-specified level of confidence or, alternatively, level of comfort. The VAR amount is found as the leftmost border of this area. The vertical line in the figure is drawn at the average or expected level of losses. In this case the UL is estimated to be the VAR amount.

An alternative way of viewing the outcome of the VAR at the conglomerate level is to look at it in terms of the "Probability of Ruin", a term which might be more familiar in the insurance sector. In Figure 4 we show the cumulative probability of firm values derived from simulations of liabilities and assets using a stochastic financial model. Some of the realisations might result in a firm with a positive net present value while others might result in a firm's default. The latter probability is given by the shaded area on the left of the figure.

The basic components to calculate the VAR are the current value of the portfolio, the sensitivity of the portfolio to changes in underlying factors (default rates, financial market prices, etc) and the potential change in underlying factors. Essentially these are bottom-up methodologies, as the risk (and capital) is calculated by first

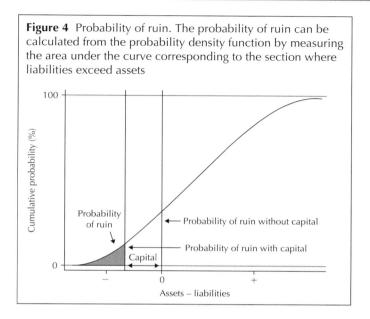

Figure 4 Probability of ruin. The probability of ruin can be calculated from the probability density function by measuring the area under the curve corresponding to the section where liabilities exceed assets

defining and measuring the risk drivers separately and then quantifying the effects of these on the entire financial conglomerate.

The value of non-liquid assets and liabilities can be approximated (marked-to-model) by the net present value of the cash flows. The net present value approach is the main basis for the calculation of insurance risk capital (UL) on the liability side. The risks arise from differences between expectations and realisations relating to the different factors that drive the cash flows. The following sources of these deviations can be quantified separately.

❑ The fluctuations around the expected value used in the cash flow projections, generally referred to as *volatility*.
❑ The *uncertainty* with respect to setting (long-term) assumptions in general (parameters and distributions).
❑ What is generally referred to as *extreme event risk*? Extreme events occur with a low frequency and a high severity. Owing to the low frequency, this risk cannot be estimated on the basis of statistical evidence dating back only a few years. For relevant risk categories it should therefore be recognised as a separate category.

The bottom-up (or risk-based) UL techniques contrast with techniques that focus on the volatility of earnings and can be classified as top-down, aggregate or index-based models. These use peer-group analysis and/or earnings-volatility analysis to determine economic capital. A major limitation, however, is that these methods do not separately identify whether the risks manifest from the loss history and, by implication, fail to provide clear guidance on how to manage risks and where to allocate economic capital accordingly. Some institutions nonetheless apply a combined form of peer-group and earnings volatility analysis to capitalise for residual business risks (see the "Business or strategic risk" section in Chapter 2).

RISK TYPOLOGY

Worldwide several institutions are developing economic capital models for banking as well as for insurance activities. Often mentioned institutions in this respect are for instance Union Bank of Switserland (UBS) and ING. Over the past few years, significant progress has been made and modelling approaches are gradually converging. In order to facilitate benchmarking across institutions, much work has also been done on developing risk typologies. Such typologies can form the basis for largely quantitative exercises such as setting up economic or regulatory capital frameworks as well as for more qualitative purposes such as supporting a risk-oriented on-site supervisory process. While there appears to be a fair amount of consensus on the classification of traditional banking risks, there is less agreement on a single and generally accepted classification system of insurance risks.

Many classifications of risk types have been drawn up. First and foremost by practitioners, who need such classifications in the daily measurement and management of risks. Once a classification has gathered sufficient support, regulators and supervisors tend to incorporate these into laws and regulations. In coming to our own taxonomy of risks, we have naturally tried to build on the existing and accepted classifications. We will introduce these in turn, starting with the banking side.

On the banking side the Basel Committee on Banking Supervision (BCBS) has traditionally played a stimulating role in the development of risk measurement in banking institutions. The BCBS has recently presented a revised the capital adequacy framework, which will form the basis for new regulation in many countries. In the EU it has led to revision of the Capital Requirements Directive (CRD) for banks, passed by the European parliament in the autumn of 2005. EU member states should implement the framework by 1st January 2007. This framework entails *inter alia* separate capital requirements for credit, market and operational risk, combined with a supervisory review process to assess the capital coverage for the complete risk profile. The supervisory review process (Pillar II) will assess risks such as interest rate risk in the banking book and credit concentration risk, amongst others.

In the current supervisory framework, supervisors have also developed approaches to assessing the risk profile of an institution. A well-known example is the CAMELS approach, used in the United States, which aims to assess Capital, Asset quality, Management, Earnings, Liquidity and Sensitivity to market conditions. Other supervisors, such as the FSA in the UK and the De Nederlandsche Bank (DNB) in the Netherlands have implemented slightly more elaborate approaches.[5] Both approaches take a similar approach in which risks are coupled with controls. Given these scores, the results are aggregated to come to an overall assessment of the relative riskiness of particular institutions. This score is used for instance in allocating scarce resources. In the FSA's Arrow approach a total of nine risk groups with 45 risk items is discerned. Some of these risks are quantitative, financial risk in line with the risks classified in Table 2. Other risks are more quantitative and focus, for instance, on controls. The DNB currently uses an approach called the Financial Institutions' Risk analysis Method (FIRM) that distinguishes between matching/interest rate risk, market risk, credit risk, insurance risks, external risks, operational risk, outsourcing risk, IT risk, integrity risk and legal risk.

On the insurance side, the European Commission has started the Solvency II project. The Committee of European Insurance and Occupational Pensions Supervisors (CEIOPS), a level three committee, has been asked to provide advice to the European Commission.[6] Solvency II is intended to be a more risk-sensitive solvency regime fostering improvement in risk management. In addition, one of the aims is increased transparency and harmonisation of regulations across borders and sectors. Presently, the European Commission intends to implement to the framework by 2010.

Table 2 Summary of risk typology

Risk types[7]	Sub types	Definitions	Risk drivers	Typical measures and measurement approaches
Market/ALM	Market or trading	The risk of adverse movements in market factors (such as asset prices, foreign exchange rates, interest rates, etc), their volatilities and correlations	Equity and commodities prices, foreign exchange rates, interest rates; their volatilities and correlations	VAR, scenario analysis
	ALM[8] (including interest rate risk)	The risk of adverse movements in the prices of assets and liabilities	Interest rates, equity prices, commercial and residential real estate prices	Duration mismatch, scenario analysis (cash flow testing [CFT] liquidity gap reports
Credit[9]		The risk of loss resulting from potential failure of counterparties to honour their financial obligations	Business cycle, sectoral developments, prices of shares, bonds, other financial products, commodities, commercial and residential real estate and other collateral	Probability of default, loss given default (LGD), exposure at default (EAD), maturity, correlations, expected loss, UL, internal rating-based approach, capital-at-risk, economic capital, credit risk models
	Cross-border (or transfer or country risk)	The risk due to the possibility that funds in foreign currencies cannot be transferred out of a country	Foreign exchange rates, local interest rates, political business cycle, political developments	(See above), VAR, foreign currency sovereign spread
Life	Mortality	Deviations in timing and amount of the cash flows due to (non-) incident of death	Mortality and longevity expectancy	Surplus, resilience, solvency and stress tests, second order foundation

	Description		Measurement
Morbidity or disability	Deviations in timing and amount of the cash flows due to (non-) incident of disability and sickness	Morbidity and disability expectancy	(see above)
P&C or non-life — Extreme event or catastrophe P&C	The risk of loss due to unforeseen increase in catastrophe claims, such as hurricanes or earthquakes	[10]	Exceedence probability curves
Non-catastrophe P&C (including morbidity risk)	The risk of loss due to unforeseen increase in non-catastrophe claims, such as car accidents, fires, etc	Frequencies/severities of insured risks (accidents, fires, etc)	Frequency severity modelling, loss triangle analysis, historical claim ratio
Operational (Including legal risk)	The risk of loss resulting from inadequate or failed internal processes, people and systems or from external events	Quality of control, volume of cash flows or other business measures	Scorecards, expected and UL, VAR, extreme value theory
Business or strategic (Including lapse risk, efficiency risk and expense risk)	The risk of loss due to adverse conditions in revenue/exposure, such as decreased demand, competitive pressure, etc	Other risks, such as changes in volumes, margins and costs, strategic risk (choice of products and markets), risk of mergers, acquisitions and divestitures	Historical earnings, volatility, analogues/peers

In insurance there seems to be some consensus as to what constitutes the main risk types (see, eg, the study conducted by KPMG (2002) into the risk profile of insurance undertakings). After having taken stock of risks that are company-specific, industry-specific and economy-wide, respectively, the report identifies underwriting risk, credit risk, reinsurance risk, matching risk, provisioning risks, jurisdictional and legal risk and interest rate risk as the key risks facing an insurance undertaking. At the global level, the International Actuarial Association (IAA) was recently requested to support the International Association of Insurance Supervisors (IAIS) in developing the "Principles on Capital Adequacy and Solvency". The IAA earlier reported a survey of various risk classification schemes and categorises six major risk headings: underwriting risk, credit risk, market risk, operational risk, liquidity risk and event risk IAA (2002). Recently, the IAIS has published two papers outlining the directions of further solvency supervision for insurers (IAIS 2005A; IAIS 2005B). The "Framework" paper (IAIS 2005A) sets the long term approach to this project while the "Cornerstones" paper (IAIS 2005B) provides the principles of risk-based supervision of insurer solvency. Some insurance supervisors have taken the lead in developing risk-based supervision in the spirit of the Solvency II exercise. One such supervisor is the Dutch DNB, which recently issued principles for a financial assessment framework that aims to assess an insurer's capital adequacy in a risk-oriented way (DNB 2005).

principles

Based on these various sources, we have arrived at a risk typology for mixed financial conglomerates that is sufficiently general in nature in order to accommodate the slightly varying approaches taken by the larger, more complex financial conglomerates. The typology presented in Table 2 reflects our reading of available classifications and the extent that these classifications are used in practice. It is by no means prescriptive, but should rather be seen as providing a collective framework within which stand-alone risks and economic capital in a mixed financial conglomerate can be assessed. The risk classification in Table 2 builds upon the risk types traditionally recognised by financial institutions and their regulators. This choice is partly motivated by the observation made earlier that risk measurement typically starts rather autonomously in decentralised business lines that each individually focus on the risks most relevant to them. The approach could therefore be regarded as "piecewise" or "incremental".

In order to properly assess the risk profile and economic capital requirement of the entire institution, however, correlations and diversification across risk types have to be taken into account. One approach to do so would be to build an economic capital framework by and large "from scratch", for instance by focusing on the risk drivers and their aggregate effects across all the institution's activities. While risk types are distinguished by the manifestation of the risk, risk drivers (such as interest rates, default rates, etc) aim to identify the underlying causes of the risk. Table 2 suggests a fair amount of similarity between risk drivers across banking and insurance activities. An economic capital approach directly built off risk drivers would internalise diversification effects across risk types and would also circumvent certain boundary issues that exist between the various risk types. To our knowledge, however, such models are still in the embryonic stages of development.

As we perceive the majority of institutions to have opted for the former route (ie, incremental modelling) thus far, the remainder of this book will build upon the "traditional" risk typology presented in Table 2. After presenting the table, we will discuss each risk type in terms of definition, main risk drivers, risk measurement, and economic capital allocation.

MARKET/ALM RISK
Introduction
Market risk and ALM risk are narrowly related. Both types of risk are defined as "the risk of adverse movements in market factors (such as asset prices, foreign exchange rates, interest rates, etc) and their volatilities and correlations".

The term market risk is typically used by banks and refers to trading, usually a short-term activity, and focuses on changes in market/fair value. The term ALM risk is used by both banks and insurance firms and relates to the consequences of changes in market factors for all asset and liability items of the balance sheet.

In banks ALM risk typically refers to interest rate risks in banking books with a focus mostly on accrual earnings where long-term assets are funded by short-term liabilities. Insurance companies face the opposite problem. Typically the liabilities have a longer duration than the assets and the asset portfolio may include some equity investments. Furthermore, both banks and insurance companies have increased ALM risks due to embedded options in their assets and liabilities. This section discusses the two risks separately and describes their application in both banking and insurance. The ALM section also includes a brief discussion of the replicating portfolio concept as a tool to manage interest rate risk.

Market risk

Definition and risk drivers

Market risk is defined as the possibility of losses owing to unfavourable market movements. Such losses occur when an adverse price movement causes the mark-to-market (re)valuation of a position to decline.[11] Market risk can materialise due to a large number of risk factors, including fluctuations in interest rates, exchange rates, equity prices and commodity prices, as well as changes in volatility of these rates and prices that affect the values of options or other derivatives, as well as changes in correlations between those risk factors. The definition specifically applies to liquid, actively traded books; models for market risk in banking typically have a 1 up to 10 days horizon.

Measurement approaches

Several methodologies can be used to measure market risk. The most commonly used methodology is Value-at-Risk (VAR), a statistical measure of the potential loss that could occur owing to movements in market rates and prices over a specified time horizon, at a given confidence level. The VAR approaches can be split into two groups: (1) The local-valuation methods, including the Variance-covariance approach, in which the portfolio is valued once, at the initial position, and where local derivatives are used to infer possible movements. (2) The full-valuation methods, including the Historical simulation approach and the Monte Carlo approach, that measure risk by fully repricing the portfolio over a range of scenarios. Each approach is described in more detail below.

Variance–covariance approach

The main assumption of this approach is that the returns on assets are normally distributed, and that the relation between assets (correlation) is constant. For this approach you only need the variances and covariances of the underlying risk factors over the holding period. It involves the following steps:

(1) identify the market factors that influence the portfolio;
(2) calculate volatilities and correlations of the market factors over the holding period;
(3) calculate the change in portfolio value by combining a variance-covariance matrix (based on volatilities and correlations of the market factors), with the risk factor sensitivities of the individual positions;
(4) since this approach assumes a normal distribution for asset returns, VAR is a fixed multiple of the standard deviation of the change in portfolio value at the desired confidence level which can be read from the normal distribution table (eg, using a confidence level of 95 per cent, would calculate VAR as 1.65 times the portfolio standard deviation). The primary advantage of the variance/covariance approach is that it is fairly easy to compute. However, an issue is that it does not properly calculate the risk of non-linear instruments, such as options.[13]

Historical simulation approach
The most widely used methodology to calculate VAR is the so-called historical simulation method. It is a simple, empirical approach based on few statistical assumptions. It uses historical changes in market rates and prices to construct the distribution of the portfolio value changes without imposing distribution assumptions and estimating parameters. The approach involves the following steps:

(1) identify the market factors that influence the portfolio and collect historical data on each factor for a given period;
(2) calculate the percentage change in these factors over the given period and use these to determine the theoretical values of the current portfolio for each day in the period;
(3) create a distribution of profits and losses and identify the VAR at the desired confidence level.

The main advantage of this method is that it is simple to understand and explain. It captures the exact range of outcomes that have been observed in the past and it does not require any assumptions about the distribution of returns. However, the main issue of this approach is the possibility that certain market events may not be captured properly, as history does not necessarily repeats itself.

Monte Carlo approach

This methodology has a number of similarities to historical simulation method. The main difference is that, rather than carrying out the simulation using actual historical changes in the market factors to generate theoretical portfolio values, this approach simulates the behaviour of risk factors and asset prices by generating random price paths. The approach involves the following steps:

(1) identify the market factors that influence the portfolio;
(2) use a random number generator to generate theoretical changes in the values of each market factor;
(3) create a distribution of profits and losses and identify the VAR at the desired confidence level. Graphically this is depicted in Figure 5.

The Monte Carlo approach is quite robust but requires the most sophisticated analytical systems and the greatest data collection effort.

Economic capital

Economic capital for market risk is usually based on the VAR measure, but it may be defined by a different time horizon and confidence interval. To derive economic capital from the VAR number some adjustments have to be made, for example

❏ *Confidence interval conversion.* Depending on their (targeted) rating, each institution has to make adjustments to the confidence interval accordingly. To that purpose, the hypothetical value distribution from which the VAR is derived, has to be fitted to a well-known theoretical distribution (such as normal, lognormal, student-t, etc). Alternatively, scaling to extreme confidence intervals can be achieved by applying Extreme Value Theory (EVT).

❏ *Fat tails correction.* Depending on the chosen distribution, a correction that takes into account the "fat tails" may need to be made.

❏ *Time scaling.* As the economic capital calculation is generally based on a one-year time horizon, the holding period applied in

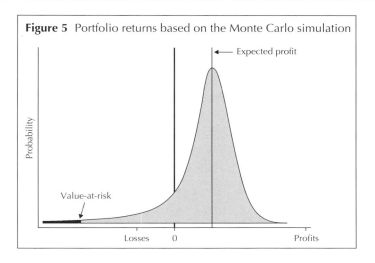

Figure 5 Portfolio returns based on the Monte Carlo simulation

the calculation of VAR needs to be scaled up to a one year risk evaluation. This adjustment assumes that daily distributions are statistically independent. For positions that are managed on a daily basis, this is probably a valid assumption. If not, errors for longer economic capital horizons can be quite significant.

❑ *Management intervention*. Large losses are likely to result in some form of management intervention to mitigate the losses from the book in question. Monte Carlo simulations may determine the risk mitigation provided by the intervention.

Asset liability management risk
Definition and risk drivers
ALM is the practice of managing a business such that decisions on assets and liabilities are coordinated. It can be defined as the ongoing process of formulating, implementing, monitoring and revising strategies related to assets and liabilities. ALM risk can be considered as the impact of fluctuations in market forces on the value of assets and liabilities or, more precisely, on the present value of future profits arising from a block of business.

In a banking environment, the structural interest rate mismatch between banking book assets and liabilities constitutes the most important driver of ALM risk. The time to maturity of the assets (loans) generally exceeds the maturity of the liabilities (deposits, other debt). This can lead to two effects.

1. Liabilities will have a shorter time-to-maturity and will thus re-price sooner than the assets. Increases in interest rates will there-fore in the short-term lead to larger increases in costs of liabilities than in revenues on assets (income effect).
2. A rise in interest rates implies a larger decrease in (market) value of the assets than of the liabilities, thereby decreasing the market value of equity. This is labelled the mark-to-market effect.

Other ALM risk drivers are equity, commodity and real estate prices, depending on the portfolio composition.

In the Dutch insurance environment, ALM risk is generally caused by guaranteed returns. Periods of low investment returns will put downward pressure on profits because it will be difficult to cover expenses and guarantees. ALM risk increases when there is a significant mismatch between assets and liabilities. For traditional life business, asset durations will generally be shorter than liability durations. It is also not uncommon that the surplus or even a part of the policyholder liabilities are invested in equities. Needless to say this increases the ALM risk considerably.

Embedded derivatives or options constitute important drivers of ALM risk, for both insurance companies and banks. The most com-mon example is a policy where the client is effectively guaranteed a minimum annual return on each premium and an option on the excess return on the asset portfolio. Variable savings accounts issued by banks contain a similar structure. Here the credited rate is more or less determined by the market environment, but there is a 0% guarantee on each deposit (ie, the notional is protected). Other examples of derivatives embedded in insurance policies are:

❑ *settlement option* – beneficiary can choose the form of benefit payment (lump sum, annuity);
❑ *policy loan option* – borrow against the accumulated asset value of an insurance policy;
❑ *surrender privilege* – allows the policyholder to renege on the insurance contract prematurely and stop paying premiums.

The following embedded options relate to both banking and insurance:

❏ *renewal privilege* – right to either continue or to renege on the agreement at the end of the policy period;

❏ *pipeline/offered rate option* – the option to determine the contracted interest rate within a certain period (eg, for mortgages);

❏ *over-depositing or prepayment option* – allows a product or policy-holder to make higher payments than required, which will be credited at a pre-specified rate of interest or used to prepay a loan;

❏ *interest rate consideration option* – during the last year(s) of the fixed interest rate period a client has the option to determine the point in time (and thus implicitly the level of the interest rate) for the renewal of a loan facility.

There is an obvious degree of overlap between the treatment of embedded options under ALM risk and the more general occurrence of lapse risk, as categorised under the heading of business risk in Chapter 2. As a practical demarcation, ALM embedded options risk is typically restricted to those lapses that can be modelled as a direct consequence of movements in market factors such as interest rates. This risk can be priced and is therefore tradable and hedgeable. Lapse risk then refers to lapses induced by all other (and often more idiosyncratic) risk drivers.

Measurement approaches
The following techniques and concepts are used to quantify ALM risk: the cash flow mismatch (CFM) approach, the CFT approach and the VAR approach. We will discuss each of these in turn.

Cash flow mismatch. The CFM approach is quantified by slotting the net asset/liability cash flows in a number of time buckets. In the banking industry this method is normally labelled maturity gap analysis. Slotting is a relatively straightforward process and Table 3 presents a simple example. A variant of the standard gap analysis is known as a duration gap analysis. In this case a net duration position is determined per time bucket leading to a total net position. The duration of the total net position indicates the sensitivity of the value of the position total to parallel yield curve shifts. Gap analysis is widely used by banks but applies equally well to insurance activities.

Table 3 Sample standard gap calculation

	Maturity period in buckets				
	0–90 days	91–180 days	181–365 days	1–5 years	Over 5 years
Assets	25	15	20	15	25
Liabilities	40	25	15	10	10
Maturity gap	(15)	(10)	5	5	15
Cumulative gap	(15)	(25)	(20)	(15)	0

Cash flow testing

CFT, the second approach discussed, estimates the earnings volatility of today's risk position based on a set of market scenarios. Possible scenarios may include:

❑ no deviation from current rates;
❑ 0.5% rise/fall of rates each year for 10 years;
❑ rates rise/fall 1% a year for five years;
❑ rates rise/fall 3% immediately, then remain constant.

Monte Carlo or historical simulation can also be used to derive probability distributions of future earnings levels. These techniques are describes in more detail in Chapter 2 under the heading "Market risk" for market risk, but they apply equally well to ALM risk. CFT is used both by banks and insurance companies. In banks, CFT is sometimes known as Earnings-at-Risk. Insurance companies may also use embedded value instead of earnings.

Value-at-risk

Finally, VAR determines the sensitivity of the overall ALM position to changes in the underlying risk factors. The same techniques as for market risk may be used: variance–covariance method, historical simulation, and Monte Carlo simulation (see the "Market risk" section in Chapter 2). For insurance operations Monte Carlo simulation is seen as the preferred approach especially when the portfolio contains significant embedded options.

Economic capital

With regard to economic capital calculations there are two possible approaches.

1. Scenario simulation approach: economic capital is calculated based on losses occurring in the case of a set of worst-case scenarios. The magnitude of such losses and their perceived probability of occurring determine the amount of economic capital. This approach is normally used as a substitute for Monte Carlo simulation in situations where revaluation of the assets or liabilities requires too much computing time. To reduce the computational burden, the number of scenarios is limited to those that are expected to determine the tail of the loss distribution.
2. Market value approach: within this approach the economic capital is derived from the VAR measure, the third measure discussed above. The appropriate techniques are explained in the market risk section and apply equally well to ALM risk.

REPLICATING PORTFOLIO CONCEPT

Generating replicating portfolios is often used as the approach to model interest rate sensitivity of embedded option products. Replicating portfolios are portfolios that replicate, as closely as possible, the interest rate risk incorporated in a certain portfolio based on actual (traded) assets or liabilities. In general, replicating portfolios are constructed for portfolios representing similar products sold to clients with similar behaviour. Buying the replicating portfolio is the best possible hedge immunising interest rate risk in non-trading portfolios. As modelling is always an approximation and hedging instruments may not always provide a perfect match, a small residual risk remains within the original portfolio. The replicating portfolio-hedge transfers interest rate risk to a different book (or management level) – normally a treasury book in a bank environment – where all interest rate risk is accumulated. At this level the desired level of risk can be determined. Risk taking in ALM terms, for example by taking a long position on long-term interest rates, normally bears the risk of higher refinancing costs in the future. To provide for a measure of control for this, a risk limit is commonly set on the risk-taking activities. Figure 6 illustrates the use of the replicating portfolio when separating interest rate risk from the non-trading portfolios to the trading or investment portfolios.

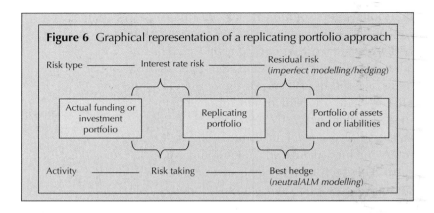

Figure 6 Graphical representation of a replicating portfolio approach

Risk type ——————— Interest rate risk ——————— Residual risk
(*imperfect modelling/hedging*)

| Actual funding or investment portfolio | Replicating portfolio | Portfolio of assets and or liabilities |

Activity ——————— Risk taking ——————— Best hedge
(*neutral ALM modelling*)

CREDIT AND TRANSFER RISK
Credit risk
Definition and risk drivers
Credit risk can be defined as the possible decline in value of an institution's assets due to the potential failure of counterparties to honour their financial obligations. Typical risk drivers are adverse changes in the business cycle, sectoral developments and – as credit risk exposure is often reduced by the use of collateral – prices of shares, bonds, other financial products, commodities, commercial and residential real estate and other collateral. In terms of assets on which institutions face credit risk, we distinguish the following risk drivers.

❑ *Loans.* In this case credit risk arises because a borrower may not be able to pay interest or repay the principal amount of the loan. Borrowers can be either companies or private individuals.
❑ *Contingent credit facilities.* These are facilities that may lead to future credit risk. Examples are guarantees (which will be invoked only when a borrower on whose behalf the guarantee has been provided defaults on his obligations) and un-drawn credit lines (on which the beneficiary may decide to draw at a future point in time). Contingent liabilities are recorded off-balance sheet as long as there is no direct exposure on the counterparty.
❑ *Traded or invested assets, such as bonds.* Credit risk is present because the value of the assets may decline as a result of an

increase in the perceived likelihood that the issuer will not be able to meet scheduled payments in the future. When present in a bank's trading book, credit risk on the assets is usually captured under market risk (as in the 1996 Market Risk Amendment to the 1988 Capital Accord (BCBS 1996)) and measured over a short time period (see the "Market risk" section in Chapter 2).

☐ *Derivatives*. Credit risk in this case only exists if the market value of a derivatives contract is positive (ie, the net present value of all cash flows owed by the counterparty exceeds the net present value of all payments to be made by the institution). Credit risk on derivatives transactions is usually referred to as counterparty risk.

☐ *Re-insurance contracts*. Credit risk is present as the re-insurer may not be able to pay when a claim arises. The timing and size of such claims are obviously uncertain. An additional complication is that the creditworthiness of the re-insurer and the institution itself may be correlated.

For most banks, lending activities are typically the main source of credit risk. Oliver, Wyman & Co estimate that credit risk is also the main source of risk for banks in general.[14] For a typical P&C and life insurer, however, Oliver, Wyman & Co attribute only 5–10% of total risk capital to credit risk.

Measurement approaches

The risk measure commonly used by financial institutions is economic capital. Unexpected credit losses are potential credit losses in excess of the expected credit loss over a specified time horizon with a high probability (confidence level).[15] Credit losses may be defined as losses due to default events only (corresponding to book-value accounting) or include mark-to-market losses as well (market-value accounting). Almost invariably a time horizon of one year is used. Institutions typically relate the confidence level to their desired credit rating (eg, a confidence level of 99.97%, corresponding to an AA rating). Sometimes institutions consider a lower confidence level (eg, 97.5%) when credit risk is looked at in isolation, while using a higher, rating-based confidence level when all risk types are aggregated.

In its simplest form, economic capital is determined by taking a percentage of the value or notional of a credit-risky asset. This percentage may vary as a function of the credit rating of the counterparty and the tenor of the asset, and can be based on historical loss experience. A drawback of such an approach, however, is the difficulty to take concentration and diversification effects within a portfolio into account. Concentration refers to the presence of large exposures to individual clients, and diversification to the level of correlation between credit events of different clients. Both banks and insurance companies therefore increasingly apply portfolio models to determine economic capital, either externally developed (Moody's KMV (KMV), CreditMetrics, CreditRisk+) or proprietary.

Credit risk portfolio models derive the probability distribution of credit losses over the model horizon using the following main inputs.

❑ Default and possibly migration probabilities per counterparty.
❑ Exposure-at-default estimate (per facility).
❑ Loss given default estimate (per facility).
❑ Market valuation routines, if credit losses include mark-to-market losses in case of downward migrations as well. Market values can, eg, be based on actual yield and spread curves.
❑ Correlation between default and possibly migration events of counterparties. Evidence exists that correlation is also present between loss-given-default and the realised default rate (higher losses per facility in bad economic times), as well as with the creditworthiness of a borrower some time before default (higher losses per facility for less creditworthy clients).

The probability distribution of credit losses is typically determined numerically, for example through Monte Carlo simulation. Economic capital can be derived as the quantile of the distribution that corresponds to the chosen confidence level minus the expected credit losses, as these should be covered by provisions. Given the high confidence level typically chosen, specialised statistical techniques may be applied to obtain reliable numerical estimates of the quantile. Sometimes economic capital is approximated as a multiple of the standard deviation of the probability distribution. The standard deviation can be calculated analytically using the above elements.

The crux of any portfolio model is the way in which correlation is modelled, and we will briefly describe different approaches in what follows. We will limit the description to the modelling of correlation between credit events of different counterparties. As the modelling of correlation is often directly related to the way in which default and migration events are modelled for individual counterparties, we will also touch upon this below.

Modelling approaches
Portfolio credit risk models can be classified in: (1) structural models, (2) latent-variable models, or (3) actuarial models.

Structural models
In structural models, default is defined as the moment that the value of the assets of a firm falls below the value of its liabilities. In its purest form, these models thus require an estimate of the value of the assets and liabilities of a firm, and how they may change over time (eg, drift and volatility of assets and/or liabilities). It is, however, impossible to reliably estimate these quantities directly from available data.

To circumvent this problem, it is typically assumed that the level of the liabilities is a deterministic function of time, while the value and volatility of the assets are derived from equity prices in the market. This uses Merton's idea to view equity as a call option on the assets of the firm with a strike price equal to the value of the liabilities (Merton 1974). Given the market value of equity, one can then back out the initial asset value as well as its volatility if one assumes that the stochastic process for the asset value satisfies the standard Black–Scholes option pricing assumptions.

The KMV model employs these ideas (Kealhoffer 1995).[16] However, KMV does not directly calculate a default probability for the counterparty once the value of assets and asset volatility has been determined. Instead, it determines a quantity called distance-to-default, which is defined as the number of standard deviations between the value of assets and liabilities. Subsequently, historical data on defaults is used to associate a default probability with the distance-to-default measure.

In this approach, the correlation between default events of different counterparties is naturally modelled through correlation between their asset returns and thus implicitly through correlation between their equity returns. Instead of estimating these equity return correlations directly for each pair of counterparties, KMV employs a factor model in which the common factors relate to geographical regions and industry sectors. By letting individual asset returns depend on the same common factors, correlation between default events is introduced. KMV distils the common factors by applying principal components analysis to historical equity returns of a large pool of individual companies.

Clearly, this approach is only directly applicable for firms that have traded equity so that the market value of equity is available. For this reason, this approach is mainly used to analyse the credit risk arising from exposures to large corporates.

Latent-variable models

Latent-variable models associate a random variable with each firm, the realisation of which determines whether default occurs within a given time horizon, or more generally, its change in credit quality. CreditMetrics is the best-known example of this approach (Gupton *et al* 1997). The CreditMetrics model associates a standard normal random variable with each firm. The range of possible realisations is bucketed, with each bucket corresponding to a certain credit quality (rating) or default. The size of the buckets is determined so as to match empirical historical default and rating migration probabilities.

CreditRiskPortfolioView of McKinsey (Wilson (1997a, b)) is another example of a latent-variable model. In this model, the value of the (unobservable) latent variable is written as a function of a number of observable macro-economic variables. The common dependence on these macro-economic variables thus induces correlation between the latent variables of different counterparties. Default probabilities are obtained by a logit transformation of the latent variables.

Latent variable models are typically used to model the aggregate credit risk arising from corporate exposures, where a latent variable is associated with each individual entity in the portfolio. Although the approach could also be applied to homogeneous groups of exposures, which could for example be identified in portfolios of loans to small firms or residential mortgage loans to individuals, this seems to be less common. For these types of exposures, an actuarial approach is generally used.

Actuarial (or reduced-form) models

In actuarial models a stochastic process for the default probability is specified directly, instead of deriving it from the distribution of one or more other variables as is done in structural and latent-variable models. A well-known example is CSFB's CreditRisk+ (Credit Suisse 1997). In this model the default rate of an individual entity or group of homogeneous entities is written as

$$p = \bar{p} \cdot \left(\theta_0 + \sum_k \theta_k x_k \right) \text{ with } \theta_0 + \sum_k \theta_k = 1$$

where the random variables x_k are independent Gamma distributed with a mean of 1. Volatility in the common factors x_k directly induces correlation between default probabilities of individual entities within a group, as well as in different groups.

The actuarial approach is often used for retail products such as residential mortgages or loans to small businesses, characterised by a large number of individually relatively small exposures. The parameters may be estimated using aggregate portfolio data and historical information on credit losses (expected loss, volatility, distribution, etc).

Transfer or cross-border risk

Definition and risk drivers

Transfer or cross-border risk captures potential losses stemming from the possibility that funds in foreign currencies cannot be transferred out of a country as a result of action(s) by the authorities of the country or by other events impeding the transfer. This includes the risk owing to the inability of a counterparty to obtain foreign currency to meet its financial obligations, and/or the risk associated with certain hedging or proprietary positions in securities of the country at risk. Transfer risk is generally related to specific economic situations in which countries place restrictions on the convertibility of their local currency.[17] Hence, the main risk drivers are foreign exchange rates, interest rates, local business cycles and political developments.

Measurement approaches

Transfer or cross-border risk measurement approaches are highly related to the way credit risk is measured. Transfer risk is measured with two separate metrics, expected transfer loss and unexpected transfer loss. Transfer risk capital is the unexpected transfer loss multiplied by the capital multiple needed to achieve the institution's desired confidence level (or rating). A similar variety of techniques for estimating underlying frequency and severity parameters (probability of countries placing restrictions, loss given transfer event, transfer risk exposure, correlations) and portfolio models exist.

Differences between transfer risk and credit risk can be found due to the following.

❑ Transfer risk default rates (ie, setting restrictions) are difficult to calibrate.
❑ Transfer risk portfolios are different in nature (few borrowers with very different exposures).
❑ Transfer severities are richer in nature. Sovereigns face a wider range of options than other clients as no formal bankruptcy process exists. Moreover, pure country risk factors (such as economic development, legal jurisdiction, etc) are generally separated from product (facility) risk factors.
❑ No transfer–risk-only models are available in the market, leading to larger differences in approaches.

LIFE RISK
Introduction
An insurance contract is characterised by the agreement that the policyholder pays an amount or a series of amounts (ie, premiums) to the insurer first and in return the insurer subsequently pays one amount or a series of amounts (ie, benefits) to the policyholder or another beneficiary, conditional on the occurrence of an event that is specified in the contract. In general, there are two types of policies: "traditional", where both premiums and benefits are fixed during the contract term, and other types where either one or both are variable (eg, "unit linked" business, where the proceeds are invested in (equity) funds). The difference in timing between premium receipts and payments of the benefits (if any) results in the requirement for insurers to hold provisions to meet the projected future policyholder obligations.

In life business the term of a policy is often one or more decades. Concluding such a transaction inherently requires both insurer and policyholder to make a number of estimates and/or appraisals of possible future conditions in order to appreciate the level of premium relative to the level of expected benefits. Some of these appraisals concern the time value of money, as reflected in the measurement of ALM and credit risk discussed in the previous chapters, as well as business risks such as lapse risk and expense risk to be discussed in the "Business or strategic risk" section below.

Although each of the above risks can affect the life insurer's financial position, it is the combined impact that matters. Adverse realisations in one part of the life insurance portfolio may well be compensated by favourable outcomes in another. The long-term nature provides the insurer some ability to smooth adverse experience over a number of years instead of being forced to account for annual achievements. Implied guarantees remain, however, so very few (if any) profit sharing systems can cope with a truly prolonged period with extremely low interest rates, as is the case currently in Japan.[18]

Mortality risk
Definition and risk drivers
Mortality risk is the risk of deviations in timing and amounts of the cash flows (premium and benefits) due to the incidence or non-incidence of death. Both in traditional business as well as in non-traditional business, insurers sell products that either provide a benefit in the case of death or a benefit in the case of being alive at some maturity date or both. As a result, insurers are influenced by both upward and downward deviations of mortality risk, particularly when the upward trend impacts a different age group to the downward trend.

The main risk drivers are mortality and longevity expectancy. Longevity is affected by the continuous improvement of medical support, quality of life and environment, safety precautions and a more health-oriented focus of lifestyle. Furthermore, insurers are exposed to adverse selection as policyholders may have a greater knowledge of their own mortality their than insurers do.

Measurement approaches
Insurance companies measure exposure to mortality risk through the use of probabilities of death over a fixed time period such as one year. These probabilities (called mortality rates) depend on a

number of variables (covariates). Normally actuaries use the gender of the person, the age and type of insurance. Other variables may include the number of years since issue date, smoking/non-smoking and some medical issues. The mortality rates are estimated from historical data. The rates are usually presented in the form of mortality tables.

The process of modelling future mortality generally starts with using historical data to develop an expected current level of mortality. Since historical observations may not always be relevant for in-force as well as newly issued life insurance contracts, it is important that trends in mortality rates are taken into account. Owing to ongoing developments in nutrition, medical and genetic science, human mortality rates have decreased considerably over the past centuries, a process that might continue in the near future.

When calculating expected mortality rates for a certain class of persons (insured lives, annuitants, pensioners, etc) the specific characteristics of the insurance policies should be considered, particularly when products include guaranteed rates over a long period such as a whole-life guaranteed annuity. Depending on the goal and the available data, several models can be applied to predict future mortality based on information about recent trends in mortality improvement or deterioration. This central projection for the future expected mortality is surrounded by: (1) volatility risk, (2) uncertainty risk, and, in addition, (3) extreme events may significantly impact the expected mortality. We will discuss each off these risks in turn.

Volatility risk. Volatility risk (or fluctuation risk) results from the random nature of mortality and the variation across insurance policies of the sum-at-risk in case of death of the insured person. In addition to the normal random fluctuations, additional volatility can result from external causes such as (extreme) cold winters or an unexpected number of influenza epidemics in a year. These can be considered as systematic fluctuations in the underlying mortality probability model. In general, the expected value of the volatility process is zero with fluctuations being either positive or negative.

Modelling volatility risk usually starts with the simplifying assumption that individual claims are mutually independent so that the number of deaths can be drawn from a binomial distribution. This assumption does not hold when people are exposed to the same risk factors. Examples include more than one person in a car accident or plane crash, cold winters or small epidemics. In order to account for this, fatter-tailed distributions are recommended, which are more difficult to model. An example of such a distribution around the number of claims would be a Poisson distribution.

Uncertainty risk. Several elements of uncertainty risk can be considered separately. First, the level of uncertainty relates to the fact that best estimates are typically derived from population or industry data. Such estimates may need to be adjusted when the insured population differs from the population in general, different products attract different groups (eg, annuities or term insurance), or company-specific underwriting has to be considered. Sometimes mortality rates are directly estimated using observations in similar product lines in the insurer's own portfolio or in (part of) the industry. Second, as the risk is a deviation from future expected mortality, the uncertainty with respect to the trend is important. The same models used in developing best-estimate mortality assumptions can be used to measure their uncertainty.

Extreme event (or catastrophe) risk. Extreme event risk is the risk of a one-time claim level of extreme proportions due to a certain event. This event will not change the parameters directly but it can be seen as a one-off shock. This kind of risk is difficult to model as there is insufficient information (a very limited number of observations). Although analysing the available information may be of help, expert judgement is typically required to assess this risk.

Risk mitigation tools
Instruments used to diminish possible adverse deviations include the following.

❑ *Reinsurance*: this can be used to improve the level of homogeneity in the portfolio measured in terms of sums at risk. Reinsurance narrows the range of sums at risk. The more homogeneous the portfolio, the less volatile adverse deviations.

❑ *Product type and policy conditions*: products can be re-designed to provide the policyholder with fewer guarantees on future levels of mortality. As an example, with unit-linked business often yearly-renewable term covers are used.

❑ *Diversification across product types with opposite risk features*: annuities (longevity risk) and death coverage (opposite risk), for instance.

❑ *Diversification across countries*: companies operating internationally and re-insurers who mitigate their exposure by operating globally.

Morbidity risk

Definition and risk drivers

Morbidity risk is the risk of deviations in timing and amount of the cash flows (such as claims) due to incident or non-incident of disability and sickness. Risk drivers are morbidity and disability expectancy. Morbidity risk exists in both the life and non-life lines of business. A wide variety of policy classes are subject to morbidity risk, including disability, accidental death and disability, accelerated death benefits, workers compensation, medical insurance and long-term care insurance.

In classifying morbidity risk, one has to distinguish between independent morbidity policies and supplementary morbidity clauses that accompany many life insurance policies. While independent morbidity policies are covered by the non-life business lines in some insurance companies, the majority of the business actually takes place in the form of supplementary clauses ("riders") to life insurance policies. Wherever the risk is classified and managed, the essential risk characteristics are identical.

Measurement approaches. Best-estimate morbidity rates are based on expected levels in the insured population/underwriting classes relative to population or industry experience and future trends. In addition to ordinary volatility in morbidity experience around the expected rates, there is uncertainty about the level and trend of future morbidity. Similarly to the case of mortality risk, calamity levels of morbidity might not be included in available statistical data. Models to measure economic capital for morbidity risks are similar to those used in measuring life risk or non-life risk or a combination of the two. Some models are specifically developed to measure the risk in disability income business.

NON-LIFE OR PROPERTY AND CASUALTY RISK
Definition and risk drivers
P&C risk comprises the risk of loss due to unforeseen increase in size and frequency of claims and time-to-payment of future claims, development of outstanding claims and allocated loss adjustment expenses (ALAE) for P&C product lines. Non-life or P&C risk is subdivided into extreme event or catastrophe (such as hurricanes or earthquakes) and non-catastrophe risk (such as car accidents and fires). While it is difficult to identify specific risk drivers, changes in legislation, technology and the social and economic environment impact the relative frequency and severity of claims within each product line.

Measurement approaches
The measurement approaches relate to the sources of risk. Sources of P&C insurance risk are as idiosyncratic as the nature of P&C insurance products. Various P&C insurance products present almost every combination of low/high frequency and size of loss. For example, in residential insurance, natural phenomena such as hurricanes are a low frequency/high severity source of risk. Another example of low frequency/high severity risk is the risk that a single product insured under a products liability policy is later found to generate life-threatening injuries for a large group of product users, resulting in significant insurance costs. An example of a high frequency/low severity risk for property coverage would be losses from the theft of radios and stereo equipment covered by automobile insurance.

Non-life insurance entities generally include various lines of business such as fire insurance, motor insurance, etc. This variety implies some diversification benefit, which may limit the overall risk for the legal entity. However, diversification might be imaginary as several lines may be impacted by the same event. A windstorm, eg, affects insured houses (fire line of business) as well cars (motor line of business).

The risk to be reflected in the economic capital is that actual variability for the future deviates from the expectations based on best estimates of the future. The total variability needs to be split between: (1) the volatility of the claims process, and (2) the uncertainty about claims-parameter estimation. In addition, particularly property claims can be split into "normal" and catastrophic or extreme event claims.

Volatility risk. Volatility risk is the risk that, given the probability distribution of total claims, the actual amount of claims will differ from its expected value. It is caused by the randomness of frequency, severity and time-to-payment of claims and related expenses. Volatility risk of a portfolio increases with the range of insured amounts, as more variability in insured amounts leads to a higher degree of randomness in the severity of individual claims. Also heterogeneity in policyholder characteristics (such as kilometres driven each year, alcohol consumption patterns, etc) contributes to volatility. On the other hand, volatility risk relative to the portfolio size decreases when the size of a portfolio is increased.

Modelling the total amount of claims can be done in various ways. One possibility is to estimate probability distributions for the frequency and severity of claims by the individual policyholders and combine them to find a distribution for the total liability. Alternatively, it is possible to estimate a distribution function for the total liabilities directly without considering the underlying frequency and severity distributions of individual policyholders. A distinction is normally made between new claims and claims incurred in prior accident years.[19] For incurred and reported claims, the frequency is already known, and only the severity and time to payment risk contribute to volatility. For incurred but not reported (IBNR) claims, there are both frequency and severity elements in the volatility. The estimation of the distribution of liabilities resulting from claims incurred in prior accident years, both reported and unreported, is usually performed at a portfolio level directly, with a segmentation into product type and/or coverage.[20] This type of modelling is more commonly used in business lines with relatively homogeneous portfolios, such as personal lines automobile, than for lines with more heterogeneity such as commercial lines liability.

Modelling should take into account the correlation between different clients. If there is such a correlation, it will cause additional volatility of the total claims liability. If volatility is modelled on an aggregate level, no explicit assumption needs to be made for this correlation. In estimating a distribution of the total claims liability based on past observations, such correlations are implicitly taken into account. Possible distributions to model the claims liability on an aggregate level include the normal, log-normal, Pareto, gamma and inverse Gaussian probability distributions. The Pareto in particular takes into account the possibility of extreme events outside of the observed range by virtue of its fat tail.

Uncertainty risk. The uncertainty risk in the P&C claims process can be subdivided into three parts. First, the parameters of the distributions used are prone to mis-estimation. Such mis-estimation can be quantified using statistical theory. Second, as already discussed in the previous subsection, the parameters driving the claims process are not constant over time. They fluctuate as a result of changes in the environment such as legislation, weather and climate conditions, rising expenses, etc. For instance, in a dry summer, there will be an increased frequency of fire incidents. The fluctuation of parameters over time can be observed in evidence of a number of a few past years. However, modelling such fluctuations ranges from being straightforward to being very complex. For instance, weather conditions can often be modelled reasonably well, but changes in a legal system cannot.[21] Finally, model risk is the risk that the chosen distribution and other model assumptions are not correct. Although it is not easy to further quantify model risk (another model would be needed for it), it can be said that some risks can be better modelled than others. Hence there is more model risk for risks that cannot be modelled well (eg, the changes in a legal system as mentioned above).

Extreme event (or catastrophe) risk. Extreme events are events occurring with a low frequency and a high severity. Due to the low frequency of catastrophes, catastrophe risk cannot be estimated on the basis of statistical evidence dating back only a few years. It should therefore be recognised as a separate category. Estimation of natural catastrophe risk is extremely difficult, as detailed and specific knowledge about the stochastic nature of such catastrophes is in most cases not known. Important, but almost always unknown information is the dependency structure between the individual risks. Due to the scarcity of experience data, the parameter uncertainty and model risk are typically large.

In modelling extreme events, a wide variety of software is currently available. These models calculate the probable maximum loss (PML) as a result of defined events given a probability of occurrence (of 1 in 100 years to up to – usually – 1 in 500 years). These models make use of experience data based on the occurrence of the events as defined. Because there are few data points corresponding to extremely large losses and because of the impact of these losses, it may be desirable to analyse large losses separately. The body of statistical/actuarial theory known as EVT provides the theoretical justification for the "shape" of the extreme tail of the distribution of losses. The theory shows that in most situations, the distribution of losses in excess of some threshold follows a generalised Pareto distribution.

Risk mitigation tools
Instruments used to diminish possible adverse deviations include the following.

❑ *Reinsurance*: catastrophe reinsurance may particularly limit the impact of extreme events, such as windstorms and earthquakes. Also, this can be used to improve the homogeneity of the portfolio measured in terms of insured amounts.

❑ *Product type and policy conditions*: products can be re-designed to include less risk or to a lower extent. Examples include the introduction of a requirement for safety measures in household policies, or the application of deductibles in policies covering windstorm.

❑ *Acceptance before policy is established*: in order to reduce the potential losses following from a policy, the insurer might, for example, test the health of a person in the case of a disability policy. Using acceptance as a risk mitigation tool might reduce moral hazard behaviour.

❑ *Diversification across product types with opposite risk features*: annuities (longevity risk) and death coverage (opposite risk), for instance.

❑ *Diversification across countries*: companies operating internationally and re-insurers who mitigate their exposure by operating globally.

OPERATIONAL RISK

Definition and risk drivers

The new capital adequacy framework for banks (Basel II) defines operational risk as the risk of loss resulting from inadequate or failed internal processes, people and systems or from external events. Legal risk is included in the definition; strategic and reputational risks are not (BCBS 2005, p 140). While developments in the insurance industry generally mimic those in Basel (IAA 2002; KPMG 2002), many insurance companies model external event risk separately. The main risk drivers are the quality of control and the volume of cash flows or other business measures.

Measurement approaches

Currently used methods to measure operational risk are based on the use of simplistic business scalars (such as revenues, funds under management), through external benchmarks, to causal modelling. Most banks, however, opt for a combination of the following two techniques:

1. the loss distribution approach (LDA), which applies statistical analysis to historical loss data;
2. the scorecard approach, which focuses on the quality of the risk control measures a specific institution has taken.

These two techniques appear to supplement each other well: while the statistical analysis of historical losses is backward-looking and quantitative of nature, the scorecard approach is composed of forward-looking and qualitative indicators. We will discuss each of these approaches in turn.

Loss distribution approach. The main objective of the LDA is to derive an objective capital number based on the size and the risk appetite of an institution and its business units (BCBS (2005)). The LDA estimates the likely (fat-tailed) distribution of operational risk losses over some future horizon for each combination of business line and loss event type. Basel II, for example, distinguishes seven such loss event types: internal fraud; external fraud; employment practices and workplace safety; clients, products and business practices; damage to physical assets, business disruption and system failures; and execution, delivery and process management.

The main characteristic of the LDA is the explicit derivation of a loss distribution, which is based on separate distributions for event frequency and severity.

The event frequency is the number of events arising from losses over a given time horizon. The Poisson distribution is commonly used to model the distribution of frequency. To test whether the data comes from a Poisson distribution, a quantile–quantile (qq) plot can be used. An additional parameter in modelling the distribution or frequency is the time horizon chosen for the analysis (bucketing or holding period). The choice of the time horizon may depend on a range of aspects, such as the length of a bad "storm" period typical for a particular loss event type, or the amount of data available over a particular time horizon.

The event severity denotes financial institution's loss in case of an event. The distribution of event severity is often fat-tailed. Unlike event frequency, event severity can normally be modelled as a continuous random variable. To accommodate the fat-tail, the severity data can be fitted to non-normal distribution.[22] A more robust, but also more complex way of generating fat-tail estimates (than only adjust for skewness), is to combine two distributions, typically one standard distribution and one extreme value distribution. The standard distribution then describes the bulk of events below an upper threshold; it mainly captures expected losses. The extreme value distribution can be a fat-tailed but flexible parametric distribution; it accounts for the truly UL.

One advantage of the LDA is that it can be applied to both an institution as a whole as well as its business units. The LDA still suffers from the poor quality and quantity of data internally available to banks, however. As the approach relies on historical losses, it does not reflect recent changes in risk profiles (rear-view mirror vision). Internal data also does not reflect the full distribution of possible events. They particularly miss out on low-frequency/high-severity (fat-tail) losses. In addition, if one then uses external data (incidents of other institutions), this data might not be relevant to the institution or might need to undergo a difficult scaling process.

Another drawback of the LDA is that, as a pure statistical model, it does not provide staff or management with tools to reduce the risk. Business units cannot change external data and if they change the risk profile, this affects the internal loss data only very slowly. To overcome this difficulty, the inclusion of a forward-looking control element in the calculation is essential. In this context, scorecards may be a useful complement.

Scorecard approach. The most widely known operational risk management and measurement scorecard system is that developed by, and implemented at, the Australia New Zealand Bank (ANZ) (Lawrence 2000). The development of a scorecard system follows a multi-step procedure.

First, the content of the individual scorecards (one for each event category) composed of forward-looking risk indicators needs to be developed. Usually an expert panel identifies the drivers of each risk category. These are then used to derive questions that could be put on the scorecards. The questions ask for quantitative data (eg, staff turnover rates), for qualitative judgements (eg, the rate of change in different businesses) or simple yes/no questions (eg, indicating compliance with certain group policies). They should cover drivers of the probability and impact of operational events, as well as the actions that the bank has taken to mitigate them. After pilot testing the scorecards, they are rolled out and filled out by all business units using self-assessment.

The strength of the scorecard approach is found in the creation of behavioural incentives to business units to manage and control their risks as a way to reduce their operational risk and to improve their risk scores. As a consequence, reduced risks will be reflected in lower economic capital allocations.

A major shortcoming, however, is that the scorecard approach as such does not give an indication of the required capital. It basically results in a relative risk comparison of the different activities. The approach requires a quantitative anchor and that is where the LDA is a good complement. The resulting capital numbers for each business units and/or risk category can then be reallocated or adjusted on the basis of the scorecard results obtained for that particular business unit and/or category.

Another shortcoming of the scorecard approach is the danger of gaming. A promising way of mitigating this problem is to focus the scorecards on quality of the risk management processes themselves.

BUSINESS OR STRATEGIC RISK

Definition and risk drivers

Business risk is the risk underlying the business a company conducts, to the extent that it includes all residual risk not covered by the market/ALM, credit/transfer, life, non-life and operational risk categories. Defined more precisely, it is the exposure to loss of value due to fluctuations in volumes, margins and costs stemming from decreased demand, competitive pressure, operational efficiency, changes in regulation, etc. These fluctuations can occur because of internal, industry or wider market factors. In one of its simplest forms, business risk is regarded as the risk that due to changes in margins and volumes earnings will fall below the fixed cost base.

Business risk can be seen as a result of management strategy and internal efficiency.

❑ *Strategic risk* is directly linked to strategic management decisions. For example, in order to realise sustainable revenue growth, management can decide to enter a new market or a new country. The corresponding risk is that the move is not successful, for example when new business volumes are much lower than expected. Another example is the decision of management not to adjust client rates in order to preserve client volume. Risks related to mergers, acquisitions and divestitures are also part of strategic risk.

❑ *Lapse risk* is the risk arising from the possibility that clients may choose to terminate contracts at any time, adversely impacting upon the company's financial position. An example of lapse risk is the loss of savings accounts or mortgage loans due to changes in the competitive environment.[23]

❑ *Efficiency risk* is predominantly triggered by the internal organisation. If a company, for example, is unable to manage its costs well, this may result in unanticipated losses if economic circumstances change (inflexibility).

❑ *Expense risk* is the risk that actual expenses adversely deviate from expected expenses. For insurance companies this risk is non-trivial, given the long-term nature of many contracts. A major source of risk in this respect is unexpected inflation.

Measurement approaches

Business risk capital can be calculated either: (1) top-down, or (2) bottom-up as we discuss in more detail below.

Top-down approach. The top-down approach mostly combines peer-group and earnings volatility analysis to determine economic capital for business risks. The approach is primarily applied in banking. Peer-group analysis attempts to define the capital level and structure required to maintain a target rating by reference to other firms in the same business. The earnings volatility analysis is based on historical cash flows.

The basic calculation framework is driven by the volatility in the P&L and a capital multiple that determines how much capital should eventually be held for a given level of confidence. In addition one can adjust for the level of (un)certainty with respect to the volatility. For the calculation of volatility, a P&L time series can be used that needs to be cleansed for other risk events (market, credit, etc). The capital multiple can be derived from so-called analogue firms. These are companies with similar activities, but without market/ALM, credit/transfer, life, non-life or operational risk. The assumption is that the actual available equity of these companies is a proxy for the business risk capital, as this is in general the requirement of the market.[24] As the P&L volatility of these companies is known as well, one can determine the capital multiple to be used to scale the P&L volatility to the appropriate amount of business risk capital, taking into account peer companies' ratings.

A limitation of the top-down approach is that it does not clearly indicate how to manage and control the resulting economic capital requirement. It may also prove difficult to find enough peers with a comparable business mix.

Bottom-up approach. Where distinct causes of residual volatility can be identified (eg, in insurance businesses) they can be modelled bottom-up, particularly for businesses that include net present values of future margins in their earnings. The bottom-up approach relies upon a detailed model that projects the future cash flows of the business unit based on frequency and severity rates affecting those cash flows. For a business unit the (existing) embedded value model can be used, and the bottom-up approach would specifically model subcategories such as (maintenance) expense risk, lapse (or in force business persistency) risk, profit margin risk and new business volume risk.

The ideal bottom-up methodology would be to simulate a probability distribution of the present value of cash flows, based on a full stochastic model of the company, using a large collection of scenarios based on coherent responses of the underlying sales, expense and persistency levels to the fundamental risk drivers. Then one could derive the economic capital from the tail of the distribution, and calculate the fair value of the business by applying some valuation function to the full distribution.

In practice, a fully-fledged multifactor model is rather complex. Consequently, a shortcut is often taken by working with point-estimates of the value distributions made by running the embedded value models at both best-estimate and "shocked" values for the assumptions. Where possible, the shocked values are derived from historical analysis based on comparable internal or external data.[25]

CONCLUSION

This chapter has provided a description of current practice with respect to risk measurement and economic capital allocation within mixed financial conglomerates. By establishing a common risk language, it has developed a risk typology that should be applicable to banking and insurance companies alike. Building on the actual experience of leading Dutch financial institutions, the framework identifies the risk types traditionally distinguished as well as their most important risk drivers.

The most interesting insight at this stage was the increased understanding of the different definitions of the risk types and how they are applied to banking and insurance activities. Even if a risk type has the same name, it does not necessarily follow that it is the same risk as definitions or risk measures might differ across institutions. ALM risk proved to be a case in point here, where perspectives from bankers and insurers deviate slightly. Whereas risk management at a bank traditionally focuses on the asset side of the balance sheet, insurers tend to approach this risk from the liability side.

Having laid the foundation of a common risk standard, a logical next step would be to consider more fundamental aspects of economic capital models. For the sake of parsimony, many of those have been neglected here. The Working Group's research agenda covered the following four main themes:

1. risk types and risk drivers;
2. one common risk measure;
3. application of models/approaches;
4. regulatory and organisational issues.

The present chapter has focused on the first perspective, namely risk types and risk drivers. The second, third and fourth measure will be covered in more detail in subsequent chapters.

The second perspective focuses on the question of whether it is possible to construct one common risk measure for a particular risk type that is applicable to both the banking and the insurance sector. Is it possible from a theoretical vantage point to merge traditional banking and traditional insurance approaches into one consistent and coherent risk measure? How do we aggregate the distinct risk types, and how do we measure diversification effects within a financial conglomerate?

The implementation of economic capital models raises a third set of issues. First, line risk managers are confronted with several stumbling blocks regarding data availability and crucial modelling assumptions. Subsequently, in due course these models need to be validated by senior management and financial supervisors. That brings us to a final set of regulatory and organisational issues, including the integration of economic capital models into the day-to-day risk management and their potential role in the supervision of group-wide regulatory capital adequacy for mixed financial conglomerates.

Authors of this chapter:
Klaas Knot, DNB; Jaap Bikker, De Nederlandsche Bank NV; Henk van Broekhoven, ING Group; Hugo Everts, ING Group; Harry Horsmeier, Towers Perrin–Tillinghast; Pieter Klaassen, ABN AMRO; Iman van Lelyveld, DNB; Raymond Monnik, Rabobank; Francis Ruijgt, ING Group; Gaston Siegelaer, DNB and Henrico Wanders, Unive Verzekeringen.

1 A more elaborate discussion of economic capital can be found in Matten (2001, Chapter 9). Another well-known reference in this field is Bessis (2002).

2 The similarity usually refers to risk characteristics, although pooling could occur over time as well.

3 RAROC is a registered trademark of the Bankers Trust.

4 See Holton (2004) for a further discussion.

5 See FSA (2003) or DNB (2006).

6 See Dierick (2004, p 27) for an overview of the (post-Lamfalussy) institutional arrangement of supervision.

7 Reputation risk is an indirect loss, driven by one of the other risk types. In principle, all risk types include the following splitting up of risk: (i) volatility, (ii) model risk (uncertainty about what is measured), and (iii) extreme event or tail risk. Liquidity risk is not considered in this survey, as it is questionable whether covering it by capital makes sense.

8 ALM includes interest rate, equity and (commercial) real estate investment risk.

9 This includes both on balance sheet credit risk as off balance sheet credit risk (counterparty risk in credit and other derivatives).

10 It is difficult to distinguish risk drivers here. "Frequencies or severities of catastrophes" would describe the extreme events, which occur in any risk category.

11 As the mean value of the assets is their current market value, the expected loss is virtually zero. In other risk classes, most notably credit risk, there is an expected level of loss (see the "Credit and Transfer Risk" section).

12 See for further elaboration (Crouhy et al 2001, pp 206–216).

13 Although techniques are available to mitigate this issue, for example Gumboll.

14 OWC (2001, Section 2.6 and Figure 2.8).

15 Unlike the market risk area, there is an expected and positive level of credit loss that would normally be (amply) covered by future margin or premium income.

16 Kealhoffer (1995). KMV, was acquired by Moody's in 2002 leading to the name change.

17 Transfer risk is sometimes also known as (in)convertibility risk.

18 See Harley and Davies (2001).

19 From an accounting point of view, pre-claim and post-claim liabilities are discerned. Pre-claim liabilities are often called unearned premiums; this relates to premiums already received for insurance cover that is still running at the end of the year. The pre-claim liability covers the remaining (estimated) insurance risk until the end of the contractual period. There is uncertainty about the number and the level of claims that will arise during the remaining insurance cover. Post-claim liabilities refer to claims incurred but not yet settled and to claims incurred but not reported.

20 Techniques for modelling volatility as a combined frequency and severity risk for individual policyholders are: translated gamma/normal power distribution, Panjer recursion and Esscher approximation.

21 The fluctuation of parameters for the insured individuals over time can also be regarded as a part of volatility risk, depending on the kind of model used. This part of the volatility cannot be diversified away by increasing the size of the portfolio as it affects all insured individuals in the portfolio simultaneously.

22 The log normal, Weibull or gamma distributions, for example. For a thorough exposition on distributions, see Evans et al (1993).

23 As explained in the "Approaches to modeling risk" section, lapses that can be modelled as a direct consequence of movements in financial market factors, such as interest rates, are included in ALM rather than business risk. After all, this risk can be priced and is therefore tradeable and hedgeable. Lapse risk refers to lapses induced by all other (often more idiosyncratic) risk drivers, including general supply and demand factors.

24 There will be some element of capital held against operational risk by the analogue companies. The capital multiple should adjust for this.

25 Due to changes in market conditions and business mixes, the accuracy of the probability distributions can be problematic. Qualitative scenario analysis will therefore be a useful addition to stochastic simulations.

3

Appropriate Risk Measures, Time Horizon and Valuation Principles in Economic Capital Models

Gaston Siegelaer, Henrico Wanders

In Chapter 1 we dealt with the question of which risk categories can be distinguished and how risk can be assessed. In order to assess the risk profile of a financial conglomerate, several conceptual issues must be captured. These are the appropriate risk measures, the time horizon and the valuation principle in economic capital models.

First, we focus on the risk measure. Given the aim of using economic capital as a common denominator within the financial conglomerate, is it possible to apply one risk measure that is adequate for all stakeholders? We identify four distinct stakeholders within a financial conglomerate: management, supervisors, shareholders and debt/policyholders. Recognising the distinct interests of the stakeholders and their views on the role of capital, we argue that the conglomerate should aim for a single economic capital model that is applicable for all stakeholders. The stakeholders face the same statistical distribution function, but are interested in different areas of the distribution function. Economic capital can be viewed as representing a common ground for the different stakeholders involved. However, to show the distinct interests adequately, the application of several risk measures may help to assess the risks from the perspective of the stakeholders.

The second conceptual issue deals with the time horizon(s) used to determine economic capital. The time horizon is defined as the length of the time period during which the behaviour of risk drivers and their impact on the economic value of the enterprise is evaluated. We propose that the time horizon chosen equals the time required to orderly cancel out the risk of the portfolio in question. The appropriate time horizon is not necessarily the same for each risk driver or risk type.

The third conceptual issue deals with the appropriate valuation principle within an economic capital model. Here we find that the valuation principle in economic capital modelling should be such that an adequate picture of the economic position of the enterprise is given. Appropriate valuation principles are mark-to-market or, as a second-best solution, mark-to-model. For risk management purposes, mark-to-model is more relevant than accrual value, even with parameter and model uncertainty, because accrual value will certainly result in a larger misspecification of economic capital.

INTRODUCTION

In the previous chapter we presented a common risk language, which is applicable to both insurance companies and banks. There we gave overview of the risk types applied in practice by many financial conglomerates. In this third chapter we consider more fundamental questions, focusing on the use of economic capital as a common denominator within a financial conglomerate. These fundamental questions are placed within an economic framework. As mentioned before, we abstain from issues involving provisioning. In the next chapter we will turn to the question of how to aggregate the measured risks.

The amount of economic capital necessary to cover higher than (statistically) expected losses depends on the financial conglomerate's risk profile. The risk profile is the net result of inherent risks (identified by risk drivers and/or risk types to whom the financial conglomerate is exposed to), and strategic choices made by its management, which may increase or reduce the impact of the risks. Therefore, risks have to be identified, and their potential impact on the financial situation of the conglomerate must be estimated.

The financial conglomerate's risk profile is summarised through appropriate risk measures. Given the risk profile and the applied risk measure(s), the amount of economic capital may be determined.

In order to discuss economic capital from a conceptual point of view, we formulated the following questions.

1. *What risk measure should we take to assess the risk profile of a financial conglomerate? One or several risk measures?* Different stakeholders (shareholders, policyholders, debt holders, management and supervisors) may have different objectives, possibly resulting in the application of different risk measures. A related question might be if and how we can end up with a common definition of economic capital.

2. *Which time horizon should be used to determine economic capital?* The duration of assets and liabilities may differ significantly between different business lines within the conglomerate (eg, trading versus life insurance), and the question arises of how this should be incorporated in the determination of the overall level of economic capital for the conglomerate.

3. *What valuation principle is most suitable for economic capital modelling?* In practice, distinct valuation principles, such as accrual value, or fair value could be applied. Does economic capital modelling depend on the valuation principle? If so, what are the implications? The question is whether economic capital depends on the accounting principles used and how.

RISKS, RISK MEASURES AND ECONOMIC CAPITAL

First, risks need to be identified and their potential impact should be quantified through appropriate risk measures. Risk is a concept that is given different definitions, depending on the context; an often-applied definition in the context of capital management is unexpected loss or "UL".[1] Where the expected loss equals the statistical mean of all possible outcomes, risk relates to the variability of outcomes, or more specifically, the possibility that the actual loss will turn out to be higher than the expected loss. Note that the definition of UL should cover all potential losses, including those not apparent from the balance sheet (such as a potential loss arising from a derivatives position, or a guarantee). A risk measure quantifies the potential impact of a risk. Economic capital is defined as a buffer against all ULs, including those not incurred on the balance sheet (such as potential loss arising from a derivatives position or a guarantee), at the company's desired level of comfort.

Economic capital is often determined by estimating the statistical distribution of potential losses. Given the distribution, a predetermined confidence level and a selected risk measure, the economic capital can be calculated.[2] Thus, economic capital is not synonymous to a risk measure; a risk measure is required to determine the amount of economic capital. Although the terms risks, risk measures and economic capital are used interchangeably in practice, from a conceptual point of view they have to be distinguished.

Economic capital can be determined in numerous ways and (some) disagreement exists in the market. In an extensive survey of American insurers for instance (Societies of Actuaries 2002), the authors present three alternative ways to determine the amount of economic capital generally seen in their responses. Economic capital is determined, at a given level of risk tolerance, over a specified time horizon, as:

1. sufficient surplus to meet potential negative cash flows and reductions in value of assets or increases in value of liabilities, or
2. the excess of the market value of the assets over the fair value of liabilities required to ensure that obligations can be satisfied, or
3. sufficient surplus to maintain solvency.

While answers one and three mention "sufficient surplus", answer two explicitly mentions that the surplus consists of the market value of assets minus the market-consistent value of liabilities. This will also be our starting point for the determination of economic capital. We determine economic capital as the amount necessary to cover ULs, at a given level of risk tolerance, over a specified time horizon. For our approach losses should be determined using economic value (be it mark-to-market or mark-to-model). In the next sections of this chapter, we will elaborate on the risk measure needed to quantify the level of risk tolerance, the time horizon and the valuation principles.

Coherent risk measures

In order to assess the risk profile of a financial conglomerate adequately, a risk measure could be applied. The literature advocates *coherent risk measures* as introduced by Artzner *et al* (1999). A risk measure is coherent if it satisfies the following properties:

Table 4 Examples of risk measures

Risk measure	Coherent	Violation of property
Standard deviation	No	Monotonicity
Lower semi-standard deviation	No	Sub-additivity
VAR	No	Sub-additivity[3]
Conditional VAR/expected shortfall/ Tail VAR/conditional tail expectation	Yes	
Wang transform	Yes	
Put option premium	No[4]	Translation invariance

❑ *sub-additivity* – the value of the risk measure for two risks combined will not be greater than for the risks treated separately;
❑ *monotonicity* – if one risk always leads to equal or greater losses than another risk, the risk measure has the same or a higher value for the first risk;
❑ *positive homogeneity* – the value of the risk measure is independent of scale changes in the unit in which the risk is measured;
❑ *translation invariance* – adding a "risk-free" asset should not affect the value of the risk measure.

For a mathematical explanation of these properties, we refer to Annex A. We advocate the use of risk measures that satisfy the above-mentioned properties. In practice, several risk measures are applied. To what extent do they satisfy the properties of a coherent risk measure? Table 4 outlines the results for some risk measures often applied in practice, or proposed in the literature.

For each risk measure, the mathematical definition and explanation of those properties that violates the definition of a coherent risk measure are presented in Annex A.

Relevance of coherent risk measures

In the previous section, we presented desirable properties for a risk measure. These properties may sound rather theoretical, but might have practical consequences if a risk measure does not satisfy these properties. Some of these consequences are discussed below and may apply to several risk measures. We will start our discussion with VAR as this is currently the most-applied risk measure.

Artzner (1999) motivates some problems with VAR. Apart from VAR, similar motivations may be given for other measures that do not satisfy the properties of a coherent risk measure. A potential drawback of the VAR measurement is that it may not recognise an undue *concentration* of risks. Daníelsson (2002) presents an example that shows the non-sub-additivity of the VAR risk measure, leading to the counterintuitive conclusion that the more risky portfolio is preferred.[5] For details, see Annex B, which shows a slightly altered version of the example of Daníelsson.

In conclusion, the VAR measure of risks is far from ideal from a theoretical point of view and has the following shortcomings.

❑ VAR may not perform well in case of addition of (new) risks, or even independent tricks. This may create aggregation problems.
❑ VAR does not take into account the economic consequences of the events, the probabilities of which it controls. This may neglect diversification benefits.
❑ For returns that are not normally distributed returns, the VAR is not sub-additive and thus may be a misleading quantification of risk.

Although these criticisms seem very severe at first sight, they are less problematic in practice. De Vries *et al* (2005) show that the problem of sub-additivity violations is not of great importance and that there are only two main, but rare, exceptions to this. As a consequence, worries about sub-additivity are in general not pertinent for risk management applications relying on VAR. Thus, VAR is still the most widely applied single risk measure and with good reasons. VAR provides a very workable compromise between practical applicability and theoretical robustness.

Although some other measures are theoretically more appealing, their application may be problematic in practice. More advanced measures may be difficult to implement due to data limitations and limited IT support. Probably even more important is the consideration that users (including management) have become familiar with VAR measures, which consequently have evolved into the *lingua franca* of risk measurement. For most users, VAR offers a rather convenient means of communicating about risk. As long as users are aware of the shortcomings of VAR and compensate for them through other aspects of their risk management – such as stress testing and the employment of internal limits, the shortcomings associated with using a VAR, rather than a more advanced measure, seem to be fairly manageable.

ONE RISK MEASURE FOR ALL STAKEHOLDERS?
In the previous sections we outlined the properties risk measures should satisfy. In this section we will discuss the application of appropriate risk measures for the different stakeholders involved.

Modigliani and Miller argued in their seminal 1958 article (Modigliani and Miller 1958) that stakeholders in a firm, in this case a financial conglomerate, have no preferences with respect to the amount of capital held in the company. In subsequent research the assumed idealised world has been relaxed and the existence of taxes, transaction costs, no infinite division of assets, etc, have been introduced. This implies that stakeholders care about the amount of capital held in the company.

Identification of stakeholders
With respect to the stakeholders that are involved within the financial conglomerate, we consider four groups:[6]

❑ *Shareholders* – stakeholders with a primary focus on risk-return;
❑ *Management* – stakeholders with delegated responsibility from shareholders;
❑ *Debt holders and policyholders* – stakeholders with a primary focus on solvency;
❑ *Supervisors* – stakeholders with delegated responsibility from debt holders and policyholders.

The perspectives of these four groups could be characterised as follows.

Shareholders
Shareholders evaluate return *vis-à-vis* the risk involved and compare it to the risk-return trade-off level in the market. Shareholders are the providers of capital and hence they carry the risk, although not to a greater extent than the capital provided because they have limited liability.

From the point of view of the shareholders there is a need for transparency in the trade-off between the risk taken and the return realised or promised. Shareholders compare the actual returns on their capital invested against those required, ie, the hurdle rate for the given overall risk profile. The required returns can be considered as a reward on the volatility of the returns. The demand of the shareholders is often translated into a maximisation of the value of the conglomerate (eg, by finding the best trade-off between growth, margins and risks).

Management
Shareholders appoint management to run the business. Their primary goal is to optimise the value of the conglomerate under the constraint that they maintain a required capital level, which would include both regulatory and economic solvency criteria. Although management is accountable to the shareholders, its mandate is generally so large that it can be considered a distinct stakeholder. Moreover, if the firm's corporate governance is not adequate, management might not act as a proper agent for the shareholders.

Policy and debt holders
Policyholders reduce their individual risks by insuring these risks with an insurer. The insurer can pool these risks and therefore the overall risk is lower than the sum of the risks faced by individuals. Policyholders require that the insurer maintains a certain level of ongoing solvency, such that the company is likely to be able to honour the obligations over the full term of the contract. Debt holders do not pool their risks, and they also require a certain level of ongoing solvency. In that sense, similar arguments can be provided for debt holders. They require a minimum amount of capital to reduce the likelihood of insolvency to a desired target level.

Supervisors
Supervisors have the legislative powers to protect the policyholders and debt holders against defaults. Although they are not direct stakeholders, their power and influence makes it necessary to consider them as a distinct stakeholder.

Appropriate risk measures for the stakeholders involved
Although one could restrict the consideration to shareholders and policyholders/debt holders as the two primary stakeholders in a company, we explicitly mention supervisors on one side and management on the other, because they have (legislative) powers

to affect the conglomerate's policy. In considering the question whose perspective could be chosen to analyse risks, we identify a principal-agent problem with respect to the stakeholders. The objectives of management may deviate from the interest of shareholders. The supervisor faces a similar principal-agent problem. Thus, the principal is the shareholder, debt holder or policyholder; the agent is either the management or the supervisor. Recognising the distinct interests of the stakeholders and their views on the role of capital can help in building the overall risk, capital and value framework within which economic capital is incorporated.

To further clarify the differences between the various stakeholders concerning the risks they face, and the resulting choice of the appropriate risk measure, suppose that the management of an institution has chosen as its primary goal to provide an attractive risk-return proposition to the shareholders. Then management has to find a balance between the desire to provide a high expected return by having a small capital base, and the desire to limit the risk of very low returns (or even bankruptcy, driving equity prices to zero) by having a large capital base. The actual balance will depend on the risk attitude (or utility function) of the (targeted) equity investors. Whatever balance is struck, equity investors will only care about the probability distribution of asset returns (and therefore equity returns) to the extent that losses are not so large as to deplete capital. An equity investor will not care about the potential size of losses beyond this level as this has no effect on the return on equity (which will be −100% irrespectively). This is in line with the interpretation that equity investors effectively own a call option on the assets of the institution with strike price equal to the amount of debt ("limited liability"). For the owner of a call option, only the probability of values of the underlying asset in excess of the strike price is relevant as only then will the option have value.

As an illustration, consider a simple balance sheet with liabilities of 90 and assets with a value of 100, thereby implying an equity value of 10. Then, the strike price of the option of both policy or debt holder and shareholder equals 90. The point of interest is where the value of the assets of the firm would drop to 90. At that point the equity value becomes zero while policy and debt holders could still be paid back in full. This example is presented graphically in Figure 7.

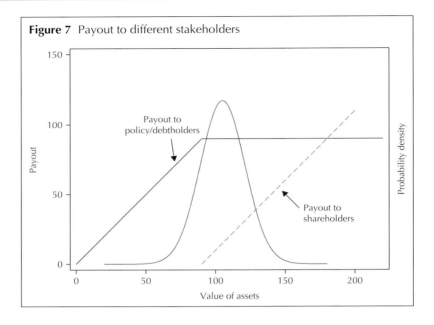

Figure 7 Payout to different stakeholders

All stakeholders obviously face the same probability distribution function, and although the probability with which the available capital could be exhausted by extreme losses is relevant to all, beyond that they differ in their emphasis on different parts of the probability distribution. Shareholders are interested in the part of the probability distribution that lies to the right of the asset value of 90, while policy and debt holders are interested in the part to the left of an asset value of 90.

If we return to the risk measures discussed in the section "Risks, risk measures and economic capital", which risk measure is most appropriate for which stakeholder? From an institution's viewpoint that focuses on shareholder value, expected shortfall does not seem an appropriate risk measure. Although VAR is typically used as a measure of economic capital in financial institutions, it clearly is somewhat awkward as well, not only because it is not coherent (under normality, VAR is coherent), but also because it implies that only the probability that a loss occurs is considered, and not the probability distribution of losses given that a loss occurs.

On the other hand, for the regulator expected shortfall could be an appropriate risk measure. The regulator's objective is to protect debt holders and policyholders. Effectively debt holders and poli-cyholders have written a put option on the assets of the firm, with strike equal to the amount of debt. This implies that they are pri-marily concerned with the probability that the asset value will drop below the value of debt (capital < 0), as well as the probability dis-tribution of asset values below that level that would determine the cost of resolution in case of default.

Thus, it seems sufficient to apply for any stakeholder the same economic capital model, leading to a single probability distribution function of losses, but with distinct risk measures, which enable each stakeholder to reflect its risk appetite in the most suitable way.

EXPERIENCES OF FINANCIAL CONGLOMERATES

In practice, economic capital is generally defined as the level of capital that is sufficient to cover potential ULs with a pre-specified probability (confidence level). In the definition of losses, all sources of risk to which a conglomerate is exposed and that can therefore lead to losses, should be accounted for. In fact, one should not only consider losses in the determining the level of (economic) capital, but also take into account the earnings capacity of the conglomer-ate, as net earnings form the first buffer in covering losses. It is thus more accurate to define economic capital as the level of capital that is sufficient to cover potential declines in value of the conglomerate with a pre-specified probability.

The confidence level in the definition of economic capital is typi-cally linked to the desired rating for the debt of the conglomerate. The desired debt rating corresponds to a certain probability of default on the debt during the economic capital horizon, and eco-nomic capital reflects the amount of capital that the conglomerate should possess so that the likelihood of default on the debt does not exceed the one corresponding to the target debt rating. As the desired debt rating may differ between the different stakeholders (eg, share-holders and management may strive for a higher rating than the minimum rating that the regulator requires) the corresponding level of capital may differ, although it follows from the same economic capital model. Furthermore, the confidence level that is used in the calculation of economic capital will depend on the type of debt for which the target rating is specified (subordinated or senior debt).

❑ If the confidence level corresponds to a desired rating for the subordinated debt, then economic capital reflects the amount of equity capital that the financial institution should possess to achieve its target subordinated debt rating.[7] The return on economic capital (eg, as measured by RAROC) then directly corresponds to the return on (book) equity.

❑ If the confidence level corresponds to a desired rating for the senior debt, then economic capital reflects the amount of equity capital plus subordinated debt that the financial institution should possess to achieve its target senior debt rating. The return on economic capital is then a composite return for the bank's shareholders and subordinated debt holders.

The confidence level that is chosen in the definition of economic capital is thus directly related to the desired risk profile of the institution (as reflected in the rating of its debt), on which class of debt holders it wants to focus when determining an adequate level of capitalisation and/or to which stakeholders the return on economic capital should relate.

In light of the previous discussion, it is clear that economic capital cannot satisfy the requirements of any of the stakeholders in full. In fact, the discussion aims to clarify that no single risk measure can. However, economic capital is relevant to all stakeholders. Hence, economic capital defined in this manner seems most suitable to present the common ground for the different stakeholders involved with the conglomerate.

Each stakeholder may obviously be interested in additional risk measures. For example, shareholders will be interested in the volatility of earnings. Management may aim for a stable dividend payments to the institution's shareholders, and thus make sure that the probability that ULs absorb too large a part of net earnings is sufficiently small. Regulators, on the other hand, may want to look at expected shortfall. In fact, the Canadian insurance supervisor requires reports using an expected shortfall risk measure, which is more or less similar to a Tail VAR risk measure (see Box). The Swiss insurance supervisor uses expected shortfall as a risk measure for setting regulatory capital requirements as well.

CAPITAL REQUIREMENTS FOR LIFE INSURERS IN CANADA AND SWITZERLAND

The Canadian insurance supervisor, the Office of the Superintendent of Financial Institutions (OSFI), assesses the minimum capital requirements for a life insurer based on a formula-driven approach, where each relevant risk is multiplied by a factor.[8] The factors themselves are the result of a stochastic process and represent the main risk drivers. In case of the default method, the supervisor provides default values that have been refined over the years. Should the insurer be evaluating a product type that is materially different from those presented in the tables, or where a company needs to evaluate a complex reinsurance or hedging arrangement, it will be necessary to use stochastic modelling to calculate factors for their particular product.

The factors should then be calculated by the insurer applying a Tail Conditional Expectation (TCE) risk measure at a confidence level of 95%. The TCE is a variant of Tail VAR. The supervisor assesses their adequacy; approved factors apply until new factors are determined or an internal model is approved by the Canadian supervisor.

Economic capital as defined above obviously uses a VAR risk measure. As shown earlier, this risk measure may violate the desirable property of sub-additivity, and hence may not recognise diversification effects adequately. Although violation of this property can easily be shown through stylised examples, it is not thought of as a problem in practical situations. Moreover, no institution manages its risk solely on the basis of VAR related risk measures. A whole host of other limitations are in place, ranging from simple bounds on notional amounts to sophisticated limit structures on the "Greeks" of trading positions. This mitigates the risk that an incomplete or incorrect picture of the complete risk profile is obtained by using only one single risk measure.

However, the fact that VAR risk measures have gained and maintained such a prominent position within the financial community shows that it is felt to provide a useful summary representation of risk in many situations. That the VAR measure is relatively easy to understand and to communicate has certainly supported its acceptance and popularity, but this alone would not have allowed it to survive for so long.

The Swiss Solvency Test for Swiss insurance companies uses the expected shortfall (ES) as risk measure for the regulatory capital requirement. ES is defined as the amount of risk-bearing capital necessary today, such that if the worst 1% of scenarios over the next year are considered then, on the average of those scenarios, the remaining risk-bearing capital will exceed the risk-margin. The well-known VAR is the threshold value for which in 99% of instances the loss is smaller than the VAR. The expected shortfall describes how large the loss is on average when it exceeds the VAR (see Figure 8).

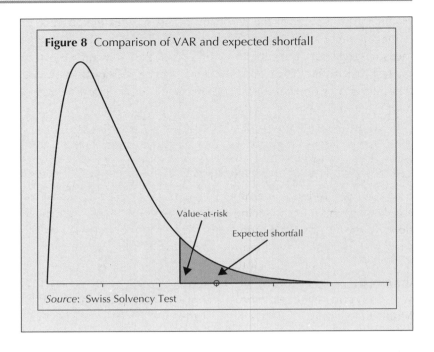

Figure 8 Comparison of VAR and expected shortfall

Value-at-risk

Expected shortfall

Source: Swiss Solvency Test

APPROPRIATE TIME HORIZONS IN ECONOMIC CAPITAL

The next question to be addressed is the question as to which time horizon should be used in the modelling of economic capital. The time horizon is defined as the length of the time period during which the behaviour of risk drivers and their impact on the available capital of the enterprise is evaluated. In practice, we often see that a time horizon of one year is used in economic capital models. Theoretically, the appropriate time horizon should be set as the time required to orderly cancel out the risk profile of the portfolio in question.[9] Note that this can either be accomplished by liquidating the portfolio or by attracting more capital.

The following example may illustrate the given definition. Current banking regulations for the calculation of market risk in the trading book assumes a 10-day holding period with no management intervention, and closing out all positions in the trading book at market prices on the 10th day. It is implicitly assumed that it could take 10 days before all positions are closed out at market prices.

Sometimes the time horizon in ALM models is set at the maturity of the contracts. This approach is called a "run-off" approach. This means that a run-off of the company is assumed in the absence of management or supervisory intervention. In that case, the risk that is measured relates to the situation when the money has run out before the last deposit holder or policyholder has been paid out. Assuming that interim positions of the balance sheet, ie, before maturity, do not matter to the behaviour of management or deposit holders and policyholders, the valuation principle does not play a role. Compared to the aforementioned approach, this approach can, however, be regarded as highly hypothetical to most companies that operate in a competitive environment. Only institutions that have an "eternal time horizon" due to government regulation or other monopolistic entitlements might convincingly argue that interim financial positions do not matter. Even then, however, a supervisor (if no one else, such as shareholders) will require appropriate actions to be taken.

Other institutions use a longer time horizon because in that case the results are better suited for an analysis of inter-temporal aspects, such as regime changes, management actions and business cycles. More importantly, it allows for a better match with the option to attract capital in order to bring the capital buffer in line with the (unchanged) risk profile. Attracting external capital is a process that generally needs a longer time horizon than a single year.

The arguments in favour and against can be summarised in Table 5. On the one hand, institutions use a one-year horizon where the risk

Table 5 One-year *versus* multi-period time horizon

Horizon	In favour	Against
One-year	❑ Simple, transparent ❑ Consistent with budgeting cycle ❑ Consistent with most regulatory risk-based "standard" models	❑ Does not accurately reflect time- or path-dependent risks ❑ It is hard to model structural changes that take a number of years to emerge
Multi-period	❑ Better understanding of dynamic, path-dependent exposures ❑ Allows for inter-termporal analysis of, for instance, business cycles, regime changes and management actions	❑ Sensitive to assumptions ❑ More complex modelling and thus increased model risk ❑ Computationally complex

is generally measured using a VAR-like measure. Alternatively, firms use a multi-year horizon where risks are modelled and measured over many periods. In this approach, for instance, the probability of default over the next 20 years is estimated.

The appropriate time horizon is not necessarily the same for each risk driver or risk type. It can be argued that the time horizon for illiquid instruments, such as bank loans, should be longer than for liquid instruments, such as the trading book of a bank. The longer the time horizon, the larger is model uncertainty and the impact of the assumptions regarding management intervention. Therefore, in order to calculate economic capital numbers, most practitioners hesitate to use very long time horizons. The possible difference between time horizons for different instruments leads to the question as to how these time horizons can be compared. Should different time horizons be scaled up to the lowest common multiple? In principle, we do not think so. Using different time horizons for different instruments can be a perfectly consistent way of modelling the possible behaviour of the company's available capital in a fully integrated stochastic economic capital model that covers all risk drivers and instruments. However, in most practical applications of economic capital models, different risk types are modelled separately and so one has to aggregate over different risk types and therefore has to use a common denominator of the possibly different time horizons.

In practice, both firms and regulators take a more or less pragmatic stance regarding the appropriate time horizon. In many economic capital models a one year period is chosen so this is the time period corresponding to the annual planning and control cycle of the company and also the time period between the subsequent annual accounts. Furthermore, as most economic capital models use VAR as the risk measure for a one-year period, these models are relatively easily understood and communicated even when the audience is relatively inexperienced in the field of risk modelling.

VALUATION PRINCIPLES

The valuation principles used in economic capital modelling should be chosen in such a way that an adequate picture of the economic position of the company is given. Assuming that the company can carry out any (financial) transaction at market prices, the appropriate valuation principle in economic capital modelling is fair value.

Sometimes it is argued that the valuation principle for insurance liabilities does not play any role. This is true for the run-off approach, but it is not true for the other situations described. In order to define what is meant by "zero available capital" with a time horizon shorter than the maturity of the insurance liabilities, one has to value the balance sheet items at this time horizon. Notice, however, that we face an intriguing paradox here, as mentioned by Froot and Stein (1998): the core of the business (of banks and insurance companies) is difficult to value on fair value basis due to a lack of a liquid secondary market in insurance liabilities and loan portfolios. This makes valuation of banks' and insurers' balance sheets at intermediate moments a difficult exercise.

Furthermore, we conclude that the basis for valuation in economic capital models should be preferably mark-to-market, although market prices are in many cases not available. A second-best solution might be to mark-to-model. The consequence of mark-to-model valuation is that parameter uncertainty and model uncertainty are introduced. However, from the viewpoint of economic capital determination, marking-to-model still is preferable above accrual value. With mark-to-model you may either overestimate or underestimate the true potential change in value, but that is still better than assuming no potential change in value. Accrual valuation may therefore lead to larger mis-specifications of economic capital.

One has to bear in mind that the choice of accrual value instead of fair value as a valuation principle can have consequences for determining the amount of economic capital. For example, consider a bank that has provided a 5-year loan of 100 to a company, and funded itself with 95 of floating-rate debt and 5 equity capital. Now suppose that because of interest and/or credit spread changes, the fair value of the loan drops to 94. Although the bank does not get in direct financial problems as long as the company does not default and thus it keeps paying coupons on the loan (and assuming that the loan income exceeds the funding cost of debt), the value of equity capital has become negative (the floating-rate debt is still worth 95). Hence, on an accrual accounting basis, the bank would still look healthy, while on a fair-value basis, the bank would be in trouble. The choice for accrual value can thus lead to large deviations from the actual financial position. For the purpose of economic capital modelling, the financial situation should therefore preferably be represented by using fair value.

CONCLUDING REMARKS

In this chapter we have answered three fundamental questions, thereby focusing on the use of economic capital as a common denominator within the financial conglomerate. The first question dealt with the optimal number of risk measures. The second question was what the time horizon should be and the third and final question covered valuation issues. In this section we summarise the conclusions on these main discussion topics.

The chapter started with a discussion of the meaning of risk, of risk measures and economic capital. In practice these elements are applied interchangeably. However, from a conceptual point of view, we have separated risk, risk measure and economic capital. In particular, the first question we tackled was what risk measure we should take to assess the risk profile of a financial conglomerate? Is a single measure sufficient or are several risk measures preferable?

In order to assess the appropriateness of a particular risk measure, the desired properties of a risk measure have to be clear. In the literature, the use of coherent risk measures is advocated. Often-applied risk measures (eg, VAR) may violate the properties of a coherent risk measure. Although violation of coherence can easily be shown with stylised examples, it is not thought of as a severe problem in practical situations.

Furthermore, the purpose of the measuring of risk within a financial conglomerate may depend on the perspective of the stakeholder involved. Four distinct stakeholders were considered within a financial conglomerate: management, supervisors, shareholders and debt/policyholders. Recognising the distinct interests of the stakeholders and their views on the role of capital, the working group believes that the conglomerate should aim for one economic capital model that is applicable for all stakeholders. The stakeholders face the same statistical distribution function of possible outcomes with regard to the available capital, but are interested in different areas of the distribution function. Hence, economic capital can thus be viewed as representing a common ground for the different stakeholders involved with the conglomerate. However, to show the distinct interests adequately, several risk measures should be applied in assessing the risks of a financial conglomerate from the perspective of the stakeholders.

The second question we tackled in this chapter concerned the time horizon: which time horizon should be used to determine economic capital? We define the time horizon as the period during which the behaviour of risk drivers and their impact on the available capital of the enterprise is evaluated. We propose that the time horizon chosen be the time required to orderly cancel out the risk profile of the portfolio in question. The appropriate time horizon is not necessarily the same for each risk driver or risk type. In most practical applications, aggregation over different risk types is performed using a common denominator for the time horizon. We abstained from these aspects here, as this will be discussed in the next chapter. Many economic capital models use a time horizon of one year for practical reasons.

The third and final question was aimed at understanding the importance of valuation issues. Thus we asked ourselves: what valuation principle is most suitable for economic capital modelling? In answering these questions we argue that the valuation principles in economic capital modelling should be such that an adequate picture of the economic position of the company is given. Appropriate valuation principles are mark-to-market, or as a second-best solution, mark-to-model.

Mark-to-model is more relevant than accrual value, even with parameter and model uncertainty because accrual valuation will certainly result in a larger mis-specification of economic capital. Therefore, the financial situation should preferably be represented by using fair value.

Authors of this chapter:
Gaston Siegelaer, DNB and Henrico Wanders,
Unive Verzekeringen.

1   See Holton (2004) and the references therein for a more extensive definition of risk.
2   Another way to determine economic capital is by means of utility theory (see also Yamai and Yoshiba 2002). Both risk and impact can be described as a utility function. If a distribution function is projected on the shape of the utility function, the amount of economic capital can be determined.

3   See Daníelsson *et al* (2005) who argue that for practical applications, VAR can be considered sub-additive.

4   If the fourth property, translation invariance, is relaxed, then the measure satisfies the properties of an insurance risk measure (Jarrow 2002). See also Annex A.

5   Boyle *et al* (2005) present a different example where a trader can make one million with over 99% probability and still meet the VAR constraint.

6   Of course, other stakeholders within the financial conglomerate are involved, such as personnel, suppliers, etc. Here we abstract from these types of stakeholders.

7   In banking, this is known as "Tier 1" capital. Subordinated debt is termed "Tier 2" capital.

8   See Brender (2002) for further details.

9   Paraphrased from the IAA (2003) "[. . .] a holding period (time horizon) for risk assessment which corresponds to the longest period of time required for an orderly disposition of the portfolio in question in order to unwind the positions."

4

Diversification and Aggregation of Risks in Financial Conglomerates

Hugo Everts, Hartwig Liersch

Earlier chapters dealt with the question of which risk categories can be distinguished and how risk can be assessed.[1] In order to determine aggregate economic capital for a financial institution, stand-alone economic capital numbers need to be combined in some way. The simple sum of stand-alone economic capital numbers of all units is an overestimation of the capital that is required at the aggregate level since it is highly unlikely that all worst-case scenarios will materialise at the same time. The difference between this simple sum and the true aggregated capital is the diversification benefit.

In investment theory, diversification means that a portfolio of risky investments will be less risky (as measured by, eg, standard deviation or VAR) compared with the level of risk of the individual investments, due to the correlation structure of the investments. However, the accurate determination of diversification benefits is fraught with problems, as these benefits are least likely to be there when you need them most. The presence of diversification does not mean that events that have little or no correlation cannot happen at the same time. High losses in times of stress typically occur when imperfectly correlated loss events do happen at the same time. Crucially, required capital levels are determined for exactly such periods of stress and consequently measurement and modelling of correlation is paramount. Since theoretically correct measurement methods are very difficult to implement and/or parameterise within a financial conglomerate (due to the large number of diverse risk drivers), in practice a pragmatic approach is taken by breaking the problem down into smaller parts. These smaller parts are easier to assess and next have to be aggregated.

The work done by the working group leads to the following conclusions.

1. The diversification effect within a financial conglomerate largely depends on the specific correlation values of all acknowledged risk drivers. Recognising diversification effects only makes sense if concentration and granularity are taken into account as well. Moreover, the measurement of diversification should take into account the increase in correlation that may occur during times of stress.

2. The current "best practice" approach to calculate the diversification effect is to first aggregate risk types across the bank and the insurance parts of the institution and then to aggregate risk types on a group level. This approach focuses on underlying risk drivers and thus on the crucial issue that the same risk is treated equally whether it occurs in banking or insurance. An aggregation approach that only at a final stage tries to assess the diversification benefit of combining bank and insurance activities in a single firm cannot properly capture the underlying risk fundamentals. Accurately capturing these risk fundamentals is essential for estimating diversification benefits.

3. Especially in the area of market risk/ALM, the combination of bank and insurance may potentially lead to substantial exposure offsets (or "netting"), that occur when we have opposite sensitivities to the same risk driver. Further diversification benefits may occur due to imperfectly correlated risk drivers. Other clear benefits could come from diversifying the systematic risk of different businesses or strategies. Such benefits, however, depend of estimating firms' sensitivities to individual risk factors and consequently a "one-size-fits-all" assessment is infeasible.

4. Actual calculations by the industry should provide an answer to the magnitude of the diversification effect, where the specific situation and outcome will differ from institution to institution. Oliver, Wyman & Co estimate a diversification effect between the bank and insurance parts of a conglomerate to be between 5 and 10%

(OWC 2001). This effect refers to an ultimate aggregation step between the economic capital of insurance and banking (and diversification between risk types is already realised on banking and insurance level). The fact that some risk drivers are unique to either banks or insurers and the observation that the sensitivity of bank and insurance to common risk drivers can differ considerably, may indicate that diversification benefits are, at least potentially, more substantial.

5. Until now, an industry standard still has to emerge from the variety of models and approaches in use. Proper measurement approaches should also consider estimation errors for data and model mis-estimation. In the long run, it is desirable to assess the risks of bank and insurance simultaneously. This creates a tendency towards integrated central risk management, since only integrated risk management is capable of revealing the full diversification benefits. Supervisors, at the same time, are increasingly relying on internal risk assessment and consequently are likely to move towards the evaluation of single, firm-wide integrated risk measures.

INTRODUCTION

The focus of our analysis is the determination of economic capital, defined as the capital that covers the potential value loss based on the inherent risks and desired level of comfort of an institution. In our analysis we will concentrate on the determination of economically required capital. The aspect of potential interaction of economic with regulatory capital, required by the regulator, will be addressed later in Chapter 6. Therefore, we abstract in the following from issues regarding the exact definition and eligibility of different buffers and its interaction with accounting treatment. Furthermore, our analysis is built on the previous chapters that dealt with the question of which risk categories can be distinguished and how risk can be assessed.

In order to determine the aggregate economic capital for a financial institution, stand-alone economic capital numbers need to be combined. The simple sum of the stand-alone economic capitals of all units will most probably overestimate the capital that is required at the aggregate level since it is highly unlikely that all worst-case scenarios will materialise at the same time. The difference between this simple sum and the true aggregated capital is called the diversification benefit.

In this chapter we will analyse the theoretical and practical considerations of measuring diversification (correlation), in particular between bank and insurance activities. In "Correlation, netting, concentration and granularity" we will first elaborate on some aspects of diversification – correlation structure, netting effects, concentration and granularity – before we move to the general measurement approaches in "Measurement approaches": a statistical approach and scenario analysis. In "Aggregation approaches" we explain that the modelling of correlation effects is, in practice, often broken down into smaller parts before these parts are again aggregated to top-level. The two basic approaches of aggregation, ie, intra- and inter-risk diversification, are specified in "Estimation of diversification effects". "Allocation" deals with problems of allocation of diversification benefits to business units/entities at lower levels, while "Data quality mis-estimation" addresses issues with regard to data quality and mis-estimation. Lastly, in "Regulatory considerations", we discuss some considerations on diversification benefits from the supervisory perspective.

CORRELATION, NETTING, CONCENTRATION AND GRANULARITY

In investment theory, diversification means that a portfolio of risky investments will have a lower risk (eg, as measured by standard deviation or VAR) compared with the simple sum of the risks of the individual investment titles, due to their *correlation structure*. Based on the correlation/covariance structure of the investments, risks can be mitigated. The remaining risk of the portfolio that cannot be "diversified away" is called systematic risk.

Correlation is thus crucial to the determination of diversification benefits. Aggregate capital will only equal the sum of stand-alone capital numbers if positions are perfectly correlated in times of stress. Since perfectly correlated risk drivers are rare, some diversification benefit will result in most cases. Generally – if risk exposures are in the same direction – it holds that the lower the correlation between risk drivers, the higher the diversification benefits. When correlation coefficients are negative, the aggregate capital required for two individual positions will be lower than the capital required for either position on a stand-alone basis.

CORRELATION OVER TIME

Correlation is one of the central concepts in risk management, expressing the dependencies between different risk drivers and is subsequently used to derive an optimal portfolio selection, for example. However, correlation is also a concept causing a lot of misunderstanding and confusion. There are two major reasons for this: firstly, the crucial assumption behind the practical use of correlation for diversification is that returns are multivariate normally distributed. Thus, from a theoretical point of view, correlation is just one particular concept to measure stochastic dependency under this specific assumption. However, for non-normal distributions with fat-tails and/or a strong skew there are other dependency measurements, for example copulas used for non-linear derivatives in credit risk (Kiesel and Schmidt (2004), also see the discussion on copulas below). The second feature of correlation that often leads to confusion is the fact that the correlation is not stable over time but can vary substantially. As an illustrative example we have plotted in Figure 9 the Dow Jones and the five-year euro interest rate (zero mid-rate) in the time period from January 1993 to January 2005.

Figure 9 Correlation between the Dow Jones index and euro interest rates

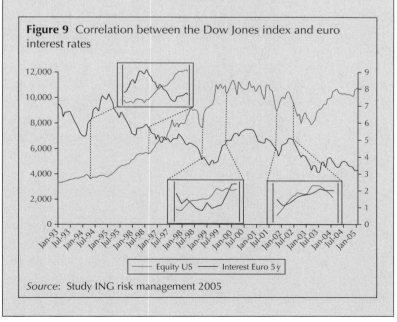

Equity US ———— Interest Euro 5 y

Source: Study ING risk management 2005

83

The correlation of the monthly returns based on the entire period is close to zero. However, by visual inspection alone one can already tell that the dependency between the two series in the first half of the period is negative (−10%) while in the second half correlation is positive (+15%). Correlation outcomes show even more fluctuations in case we zoom in on three specific periods. In the period March 1995 to August 1996 ("Tequila crises"), correlation is substantially negative (−30%), whereas under the more extreme emerging market crises (September 1998–September 1999) and the terrorist attack in New York (October 2001–June 2002) the correlation is the highest (approximately 25%). To (partly) capture the behaviour of the correlation measure, risk managers commonly use correlation under extreme circumstance, so-called tail-correlation, to aggregate economic capital.

The presence of diversification does not mean that events that have little or no correlation cannot occur at the same time. High losses, such as in the Asia crisis (1997) and Long Term Capital Management (LTCM) (1998) crises, typically occur when normally imperfectly correlated loss events happen at the same time. Moreover, correlation between risk drivers may increase in bad economic times (as has been evidenced for stock price returns). Using an average correlation that does not take into account the increase in correlation that may occur in times of stress would result in underestimating the default risk of the institution.

Whereas correlation can only occur between risk drivers, diversification will also arise due to off setting exposures, so-called netting. As in this instance risk exposures on the same risk driver point in different directions, it holds that, contrary to the statement above, the higher the correlation the higher the netting effect.

An adequate economic capital framework will accurately capture these netting effects and the resulting diversification that arises. Such hedges arise because institutions simultaneously have exposures with opposite risk profiles, ie, have an opposite reaction to the same risk driver(s). The familiar aggregate example is the life insurer taking on long-term obligations with shorter-term assets. Banks generally have a reversed profile since deposits (ie, liabilities) are short termed whereas assets typically have a much longer maturity (for more details on this see " Market risk").

Diversification benefits will be smaller if there is a *concentration* of similar risk exposures in different businesses. Concentration risk is the risk resulting from a large exposure to a common risk driver, or large exposures to highly correlated risk drivers. Measuring risks in a similar way across the banking and insurance parts of an institution will facilitate identifying such concentration risks.

Another aspect related to the magnitude of diversification benefits is *granularity*. The level of granularity is determined by the number of risk positions in a portfolio or business unit on the one hand, and their relative sizes on the other. The larger the number of risk positions, and the more equal they are in size, the more granular a portfolio is, and the larger diversification benefits will be.

In many simulation models, such as the historical simulation method used to calculate solvency capital for market risk, granularity in the risk positions will directly be taken into account. Some risk models, for example the internal rating-based model underlying the Basel II capital requirements, are only valid theoretically when the risk positions of portfolios are infinitely fine grained. In practice, such models work reasonably well with a moderately large number of risk positions, ie, a couple of thousand (note that risk positions do not refer to the number of business units, but to individual exposures such as loans). These models become more accurate as the number of positions in a portfolio increases and granularity is an indication of the effective number of risk positions. The extent to which model outcomes may be biased due to limited granularity is called the granularity effect. This effect may be particularly pronounced for smaller and concentrated institutions and for institutions with relatively concentrated risk positions to single counterparties, which reduces the effective number of risk positions.[2] Note that granularity is required to fully diversify a portfolio and be left with only systematic risk (ie, to get rid of idiosyncratic risk of each risk position).

The relative sizes of risk positions within an institution/portfolio have a major influence on diversification; eg, the aggregate firm diversification benefits between a small bank and a big insurance firm tend to be smaller than aggregate diversification benefits of an institution where bank and insurance are of equal size. A simple example: assume a small bank with economic capital of 1 and big insurance with economic capital 9. In this case correlation is 0, the total economic capital is slightly higher than 9 and diversification is less than 10%. However, in the case where the bank and insurance are equally sized with an economic capital of 5 each and no correlation is assumed, their total capital is approximately 7 and diversification benefit is 30%. If this effect is not accommodated in the aggregation of risk, diversification benefits may be under- or overestimated.

MEASUREMENT APPROACHES

A general approach to quantifying the diversification effect is to simultaneously model the correlation between all relevant risk drivers at all possible aggregation levels.

For example, each business line may be assessed on the basis of its sensitivity to changes in the dollar/euro exchange rate. These sensitivities can be summed to provide a firm-wide assessment of the aggregate firm sensitivity to this exchange rate. At both the business unit level and at the aggregate level, such sensitivities could be fed into a VAR or stress test model to determine the amount of economic capital corresponding to this exposure. Importantly, if some business units are positively exposed to increases in the value of the dollar, while others are negatively exposed, the aggregate economic capital for this risk will be less than the sum of the individual business unit calculations (ie, netting).

Following through on this approach would result in each business being assigned a set of risk drivers, some of which will relate to market risk, some to credit risk, some to operational risk, and so on. Sensitivities to each of the risk drivers can be added up across all business units. The various risk drivers can be aggregated to arrive at an overall economic capital estimate by assessing the variability of risk drivers and correlation values between them.

The most straightforward measurement of risk starts at the lowest level where information is available that covers all relevant parameters and exposures to different risk drivers for the considered activity. By starting bottom-up one does not need to define the correlation between higher-level risk types, for example the general correlation between credit and market risk, or between two business units since they are implied by the correlation between the lower level risk drivers.

In practice, two methods are generally used to assess diversification effects:

❑ the statistical approach – a quantitative analytical or numerical solution;
❑ the scenario analysis approach, which is mainly qualitative (ie, based on expert judgement or historical observation).

In many institutions, these approaches are used in combination where insights from the scenario analysis approach supplement the results from the correlation approach.

Statistical approach
The most common approach in estimating the diversification effect is to use a correlation matrix. The correlation coefficient reflects the statistical dependency between random variables. It measures the degree of linear dependency between two (or more) random variables. A correlation coefficient of one implies that two random variables move in exactly the same way ("perfect correlation"). Diversification occurs when correlation coefficients are less than one ("imperfect correlation").

A common (although not necessary) assumption is that the potential losses resulting from exposure to a particular risk driver follow a normal distribution. As a consequence, overall potential losses are assumed to follow a normal distribution as well. If risk capital is calculated as a multiple of the standard deviation, the overall risk capital is determined *analytically* by a function of correlation coefficients and the separate risk capitals.[3]

For instance, the computation behind the very simple example in the last paragraph of the previous section clearly demonstrates that the risk distribution can be fully described by a mean (vector), correlations factors (covariance matrix) and a generator function: in case the bank economic capital (B) is 5 and the insurance economic capital (I) is 5 and both economic capital follow a standard normal distribution (standard deviation = 1; $\sigma_{B, I}$), the aggregated economic capital equals 7.1 if the correlation is set to 0 (ρ). The computation is $\sqrt{\sigma_B^2 B^2 + \sigma_I^2 I^2 + \rho \sigma_B B \sigma_I I} = 7.1$.

Although calculation becomes more difficult when using more risk drivers and/or different normally shaped distribution, the main benefit of this approach is clearly ease of implementation.[4] The primary challenge is the determination of the correlation values to be used. Average correlation values may be less suitable for times of stress (see

Groupe Consultatif 2005) for an extensive discussion of this issue). For these periods, it is more appropriate to use tail or stress correlation values although these are more difficult to estimate.

In reality, the normality assumption may not hold as potential losses exhibit fatter tails than would be consistent with the normal distribution. When this is taken into account, there is usually no longer an analytic way to estimate the overall risk capital, and one has to resort to simulation. For such a *numeric approach*, one could generate, eg, 10,000 scenarios over time out of the joint probability distribution of risk drivers and the worst five scenarios outcomes determine the capital needed at a certain confidence level (here 99.95%). The drawback of this approach is, however, that modelling the joint probability distribution simultaneously for all risk drivers over insurance and banking is very complex.

Another complication is that the correlation coefficient does not always capture the total dependence structure as it is a measure for linear dependency that does not include extreme cases. This leads to a general tendency of underestimation of correlation coefficient and consequently to overestimation of diversification benefits. More general dependence structures such as copulas (see Dorey and Joubert 2005) can be used to incorporate this effect, but they are very difficult to work with in practical situations, ie, combining a substantial number of different risk distributions in a financial conglomerate. Many practitioners think that a simpler approach, for example simulation in combination with "tail"-correlation, can already provide acceptable results.

An alternative – and theoretically more sound – method to calculate diversification under extreme events is the use of copulas.[5] The copula supports the combination of marginal movements with other dependency models and is thus helpful in analysing the sensitivity of risk with regard to changing dependencies in the tail. Furthermore, copulas have the advantage that they can accurately combine other distributions other than only normally shaped distributions. They facilitate a bottom-up approach to describe extreme outcomes as they isolate individual risks from their dependence structure. Although copulas might be too complex to be used in aggregating all risks of a financial conglomerate they can provide deeper insight in dependencies under extreme events and are, eg, very useful in credit risk. In credit risk, risk managers normally

Table 6 A comparison of correlation and copulas for aggregation

Methodology	Advantages	Disadvantages
Correlation	❏ Simple, intuitive and easy to explain to non-experts ❏ Aggregated economic capital can be derived analytically with individual capital amounts and correlation coefficients ❏ *Parameter estimation is technically simple*	❏ Theoretically incorrect if the assumed (normal) distribution is not the same as the portfolio distribution ❏ *Correlation estimation using historical data might not capture "current" correlation* ❏ *Correlations might be underestimated if – due to data shortage – too short data series are used in series that are serially correlated*
Copulas	❏ No particular joint distribution of returns/earnings needs to be assumed ❏ If the right copula is used, model (and tail) dependence can accurately be captured while the original distribution of returns/earnings can be maintained	❏ Difficult to explain to non-experts ❏ Allocated economic capital amounts might be sensitive to the copula chosen ❏ Consistent individual economic capital amounts might be difficult to achieve ❏ *Choosing the right copula function and parameters might require a time series that is too long. Using a shorter time series is likely to increase model risk as choosing parameters and the copula becomes arbitrary*

Note: Adapted from Saita (2004). Italics are used to denote calibration issues.

have a better idea about the marginal movements of an individual obligor than they have on the joint default structure in a credit portfolio. Copulas are frequently used for modelling, eg, credit derivatives.

In Table 6 we summarise our discussion of the use of correlation or copulas in modelling dependencies.[6] The relative importance of the arguments in favour and against mentioned in this table will differ as the model outcomes might be used for different purposes. If, for instance, the economic capital outcome is only used for senior management's decisions on the overall capital structure and not used in an internal capital allocation process, the relative importance of attributes such as transparency, business model (fully integrated versus loose portfolio) or the ability to deliver economic capital attributed to particular business units will be different. Institutions might thus choose different methods because of different objectives.

Scenario analysis
Another approach to assess diversification benefits is to determine a set of scenarios that will provide the combined effect/result of different risk drivers. In general these scenarios are determined qualitatively through expert judgement.

These scenarios must then implicitly capture the correlation and diversification effects between certain risk drivers. The challenge of such a *qualitative approach* is to select an appropriate small set of base scenarios per risk driver, by expert judgement or reflecting historical experience, which reflect worst-case scenarios of a specific probability and then apply several methods to combine these scenarios.

Generally, the effect of worst-case scenarios with a certain probability, which is tied to some rating level, is assessed. For example, an AA rating is often associated with a default probability of 0.05% per year. Defining a scenario that has the matching probability is difficult, even more so when taking into account the instability of parameters over time. In such an environment, knowledge of the underlying probability distributions is essential.

An important consideration is to keep scenario analysis future oriented, rather than a reflection of previous "wars". Consequently, subjective considerations will play an important role, as some historical events are simply not possible anymore while others may never have happened in the past but are not unlikely for the future. Additional difficulties may arise if the diversification effects are to be assessed separately because then the selected scenarios, reflecting a 0.05% default probability, have to be compared to the normal, average scenario.

Nonetheless, the scenario approach can be very useful as a supplementary approach, for example, to identify the presence, dynamics and magnitude of netting effects or to obtain some more intuition for the results of the statistical approach.

ECONOMIC CAPITAL CONCEPTS IN THE ACADEMIC LITERATURE

The present study deals with economic capital. This is, contrary to actual or regulatory capital, the amount of capital a financial firm itself deems necessary, given its risk profile and the state of controls. As such it is not a new concept but for instance reductions in computing costs have made it possible to approach the subject on a more comprehensive and model based fashion.

At first glance, the problem of determining the optimal amount of economic capital would seem to be solved by a straightforward application of portfolio selection theory. A firm decides to combine a number of activities that interact in some sense and given their risk and return characteristics, the portfolio will, after judicious aggregation, have some risk profile. Technical issues would off course still be daunting: How would we aggregate across risks? What is an acceptable holding period? Moreover, the funding of activities would not enter into the equation and the twist is that the funding costs of financial firms, partially because of high leverage, are sensitive to the risk profile. This section will not deal with theoretical insight into the measurement of particular risks, like for instance market or credit risk. Instead we would like to highlight insights into the more general framework and aggregation issues.

One issue that is important in this respect is the discussion whether firms should hedge. Hedging is generally beneficial, if it can allow a firm to avoid unnecessary fluctuations in either investment or external funding. If a firm does not hedge, there is some variability in the cash flows. Miller (1998) advocates the use of present value as an appropriate measure for economic exposure. According to Miller, looking at the magnitude of the net cash flows is clearly incorrect when a firm's level of capitalisation changes over time. Corporate economic exposures may be unstable over time. While structural instability is viewed as problematic, temporal instability is of fundamental interest for strategic management. Therefore, the various exposures corporations face must be assessed and managed from an integrated perspective.

A relatively simple model that gives us a useful theoretical framework for our discussion has been developed by Froot and Stein (1998). Essential ingredients in their model are that accessing external finance is costly and that at least a part of the risk taken by an institution is non-tradable and thus cannot be hedged. Given that there is some cost to holding capital, risk management, capital budgeting, and capital structure policy become linked.

The model distinguishes three periods: an initial period (T0) in which the institution decides how much capital to hold, a second period (T_1) in which new projects emerge and the institution can enter into these projects, and a final round (T_2) where the pay-out is determined. In the first round the institution starts with a given initial portfolio and decides how much equity capital to hold. Raising capital at this point is costless but there is an increasing cost at the final period T_2 when a firm can go to the capital market. At T_1 a new product is introduced and the institution has to decide how much to invest in this activity. In addition, the institution has to decide how much too hedge (building on Froot, Scharfstein, and Stein (1993)). Thus the amount of cash the institution has on hand at T_2 will depend on the realisations on its old exposures, on its new product, and on its hedging positions, as well as on the amount of capital raised at T0. The reason the institution cares about the distributional characteristics of cash balances is that at T_2 there is "sure thing" investment opportunity for which some investment is necessary. This investment can be funded by internal cash or by external funds, which are increasingly costly to raise and thus the marginal value of cash is positive but decreasing. Leaving out period T_1 reduces the model to a typical Myers and Majluf (1984) pecking order model of equity. Adding period T_1 gives the institution two tools, besides keeping cash, to counter "underinvestment distortions caused by costly external financing". The institution can either adjust its risk-profile through a hedge or it can decide to be more or less aggressive in investing in the new, risky activity at time T_1. This model has the following empirical implications.

Summary of empirical implications

❑ the optimal hedging strategy does not involve complete insulation of the firm value from marketable sources of risk;
❑ firms hedge more if their cash flows are closely correlated to the collateral values;
❑ firms hedge less if their cash flows are closely correlated to future investment opportunities;
❑ multinational firms' hedging strategies depend on a number of considerations such as exchange rate exposure of both investment expenditures and revenues;
❑ non-linear hedging instruments typically allow firms to coordinate investment and financing plans more exactly than linear instruments;
❑ there is a meaningful distinction between futures and forwards as hedging tools; an optimal hedging strategy depends on both the nature of the market structure and the hedging strategies adopted by its competitors.

The fairly intuitive result emerges that if all risks are perfectly tradable, the value of the institution is maximised by hedging completely. This is a oversimplified result because it is assumed that risks are costles to hedge. More importantly, the whole balance sheet is hedgeable. The very existence of intermediaries, however, is often explained by informational asymmetries meaning that they specialise in products that are opaque and thus not easily traded, let alone hedged. To make the model more realistic, Froot and Stein decompose the exposures in a tradable and a non-tradable part. An example of a non-tradable position could, for instance, be private equity. It turns out that an institution will still hedge all tradable risks.

Subsequently, the authors discuss the investment decision at T_1. If there is a single investment, the optimal amount to invest is shown to depend on how rewarding the investment is, how much the non-tradable risk is linked to market risk and the risk aversion of the institution. If capital is infinite, the risk-aversion is not important but with lower levels of capital, the probability that the institution has to access the external market (at some cost) increases. "The greater the contribution of the new non-tradable risk to the variance of the institution's overall portfolio of non-tradable risk, the more pronounced the conservatism." Since the optimal amount to invest depends on how the investment opportunity is linked to the portfolio already held, there is no single unique hurdle rate. Only for small investments an approximation can be found.

In the case of multiple investment opportunities, the amount to invest in a project not only depends on the old portfolio but also on the link with other investments evaluated. There are two sources of interdependence: (1) a *covariance spillover* effect, because projects will become more interesting if the covariance with other projects evaluated is low, and (2) a *institution wide cost of capital* effect, because investing in a single, large opportunity might raise the risk aversion of the institution with negative repercussion for the other opportunities considered. These two effects would argue for centralised decision taking although there is a cost to this as well. Head office needs to gather data in order to determine the firm's risk aversion and the degree of non-tradable risks in the books. The central question now turns out to be not whether some centralised decision making is necessary but how often this should happen.

The authors then turn to the determination of the amount of capital the institution holds at T_0. Here it turns out that the classic Modigliani-Miller result of debt-equity equivalence emerges if there is no cost to holding capital. Introducing a cost of holding capital results in cutting levels of capital and the introduction of the risk-aversion of the institutions. Empirical evidence for the model proposed is difficult to find because (1) hurdle rates are difficult to observe and (2) exogenous shocks to capital are hard to find. With regard to the latter: in a credit crunch reduced bank capital leads to substantial declines in lending volumes, implying that capital matters for lending. However, if a reduction in bank capital is only symptomatic of a bad lending environment, then falling lending volume could reflect a scarcity of good lending opportunities instead of changing hurdle rates.

After discussing some examples, the authors compare their findings with a RAROC approach which generally consists of applying some variant of the following steps:

1. Measure the *expected return* to capital given by:

$$r_i = DCF / VaR(\alpha \%)$$

In words, the rate of return is given by the discounted cash flows (DCF) divided by the value at risk (VaR) at some α-percentile of the loss-distribution. Thus the rate of return is framed in terms of expected return in relation to the capital at risk.

2. Measure the *cost of capital* (i.e. the hurdle rate)

$$h_i = r_f + (r_m - r_f) \beta,$$

where r_f is the risk-free rate, r_m the market rate of return and β the relation with the market return. β is given by $\rho(i, M) \sigma_i /\sigma_M$.

3. Maximise $r_i - h_i$

In other words, each investment under consideration is allocated a certain amount of capital. Multiplying the allocated amount of capital by a cost of capital yields a capital charge. The hurdle rate is then the relevant riskless rate plus the capital charge. In that sense, RAROC can be thought of as a one-factor risk-pricing model.

Using the Froot and Stein model as a starting point, three weak spots can be identified. First, RAROC can only deliver value maximisation if it is applied on a post-hedged basis (i.e. not contain any tradable risk) which might be difficult to implement in practice. Second, not only an asset or activity's variance but also it's covariance with the existing portfolio should enter the equation. Finally, coming up with the correct cost of capital or relevant beta is not easy. Chatterjee *et al* (1999) for instance argue that a capital asset pricing model (CAPM) cannot model all risks realistically, as: (1) it is not possible to construct a full diversified portfolio, (2) markets are subject to a host of information asymmetries, (3) investors care about more than just beta (systematic risk), for example, the firm's unsystematic risk might be a key predictor. On the other hand, according to the well-known Modigliani–Miller paradigm, buying and selling options cannot alter the company's value.

A more practical criticism is voiced by Robinson (2001): decisions based on this framework are arbitrary because the VaR(α %)-amount is very sensitive to the choice of α in combination with the actual loss-distribution. The shape of the tail of the distribution differs significantly between different sort of returns and raising α will thus have significant effects on the relative r_i's. This in turn might change depending on which projects eventually pass the hurdle rate.

In conclusion, the model presented by Froot and Stein (1998) is a concise model in which the capital budgeting and risk management within a institution is given a firmer theoretic footing. Contrary to Modigliani-Miller there is a reason to manage the riskiness of an institution. An essential point in their story is that each investment decision will affect the (optimal) capital structure, which in turn influences the hurdle rate the particular investment has to pass. This point gains in importance for financial conglomerates because risks are more diverse and the total risk thus more unpredictable. Although it is infeasible to determine the impact of each individual investment on the hurdle rate, such feedback effects should be incorporated in case investments are large, in particular if covariance with the existing portfolio is large. For day to day pricing decisions, however, calculating a feedback effect is impractical and not likely to have a significant impact.

Separate from these recent developments difficulties arise because we want to aggregate *across types of risks* and *across types of business units or institutions*. At many institutions risk measurement and management started as a bottom-up approach (as discussed in the chapter Risk Measurement within Financial Conglomerates). An individual unit would develop risk measurement systems to capture the prime risk that unit is facing: market risk for a trading desk, credit risk for a unit involved in lending and interest rate risk for an ALM-unit. Such a risk-by-risk has resulted in a patchwork of differing approaches making aggregating across risks difficult. Similarly to the problems with aggregating across risks, there are challenges in aggregating across types of businesses because the focus of risk measurement is quite different: banks generally stress the risks on the asset side of the balance sheet (credit risk) and, to a lesser extent, from the interaction between the two sides of the balance sheet and/or off-balance sheet items (interest rate risk, liquidity risk). In insurance, however, the focus is on the risk arising from the liability side (mortality risk, catastrophe risks) (Cumming and Hirtle 2001). To date, however, there is a lack of work on how to come to such an aggregate measurement although the Froot and Stein model tells us that interaction between risks is important. Obviously, standardising risk measurement on the lower level will improve the quality of the overall measurement.

AGGREGATION APPROACHES

Due to the large number of (diverse) risk drivers within a financial conglomerate it is very difficult to model diversification with the measurement methods described in the previous section. These risk drivers range from "pure" financial drivers like for example movements in the stock markets for a trading position within market risk to the number of employees working in controlling driving the operational risk for process failure. In practice the problem is often broken down into smaller parts where the correlation of risks can be addressed in a theoretically correct manner and then these parts are again aggregated to top-level. This approach allows for tailor-made risk measures, in order to accommodate variously shaped risk distributions. The different risks then have to be aggregated to a composite picture. Economic capital does provide such a "common currency" for risk aggregation as discussed in Chapter 4.

Usual practice for a stand-alone bank or insurance company is that the parameters that determine sensitivity to a risk driver for market risk is input into a market risk, economic capital model. Similarly, the parameters for the other risks discerned are fed into their respective economic capital models. The result is a firm-wide measure of economic capital for market risk, a firm-wide measure of economic capital for credit risk, etc. Similar calculations can also be repeated at the individual business unit level, but again the result will be separate measures of economic capital by risk type. The final question in the aggregation problem is then how to aggregate measures of economic capital across risk types.

In general, two aggregation approaches can be applied to arrive at an overall economic capital estimate at group level.

1. First, aggregate across risk types within the bank and the insurance firm and then aggregate the total economic capital for both the insurance firm and bank at group level.
2. First, aggregate by risk type across bank and insurance. Then subsequently aggregate risk types at the group level.

The choice of approach to aggregation depends on information and data consistency. Obviously, data consistency is a pre-requisite for robust aggregation. In a robust diversification model the total diversification effect should not be sensitive to the order in which items are added or whether items have first been clustered. Yet in practice, the quality and degree of integration of the available data is crucial in how aggregation is performed across banking and insurance.

Notwithstanding the intuitive appeal of the second approach, firms may use the first approach because of practical considerations, for example organisational or managerial structure. Yet, the second approach currently seems to be best practice in the industry as its application is more clear-cut. The approach is more consistent and fewer assumptions are necessary as it focuses on underlying risk drivers and thus on the crucial issue that the same risk should be treated equally regardless whether it occurs in banking or insurance.

ESTIMATION OF DIVERSIFICATION BENEFITS

Before describing the best practice approach of aggregation and discussing the potential diversification benefit between banking and insurance we shortly define the two major levels of diversification, which are also the steps of aggregation as described above.

1. Diversification within a risk type (intra risk), for example market risk diversification between bank and insurance.
2. Diversification between risk types (inter-risk), for example between market and credit risk. Again the focus is on possible diversification benefits between bank and insurer.

We will discuss each of these levels in turn.

Intra risk diversification

The intra risk diversification reflects the level of diversification within a single risk type. We will first briefly describe all risk types and then focus on possible diversification benefits between banking and insurance activities by risk type. For a detailed description on modelling and measuring economic capital by risk type we refer to Chapter 2.

Market/ALM risk

Market/ALM risk is described as the risk of adverse movements in market factors, ie, asset prices, interest rates or foreign exchange (FX) rates, etc. The term market risk is typically used by banks and refers to trading – usually a short-term activity. The term ALM risk is used by both banks and insurance firms and relates to the consequences of changes in market factors for all assets and liabilities of the balance sheet. ALM risk is typically a substantial risk in terms of economic capital for both banking and insurance. Consequently, any diversification benefits within ALM can have a significant effect on the aggregate economic capital level for ALM/market risk.

Usually insurance firms are – to a greater or lesser degree – exposed to the whole range of market factors, whereas banks market risk is normally concentrated within interest rate risk (ALM). Diversification benefits between bank and insurer emerge when interest rates (ALM risk of bank) are not fully correlated with other risk drivers such as movements in stocks or real estate prices (market risk of insurer). Insurance firms typically face more real estate and equity risk than banks and thus they are more sensitive to stock (and real estate) market movements. As correlation values between different risk drivers are generally below 1, this certainly produces some diversification benefits. Of course, the extent to which diversification benefits between banks and insurance firms are present depends on the composition of the exposures across markets. It is clear, however, that the source of the diversification benefit is a less-than-perfect correlation between different risk drivers.

A different kind of diversification effect is solely related to the interest rate risk exposures. In general, interest rate risk is a dominant risk factor for ALM risk in both industries. Yet, it is not correlation causing diversification but offsetting risk exposures so that the netted position has lower risk than the sum of two separate positions.[7] In terms of exposure to interest-rate risk, banks typically have long-term assets (loans) and short-term liabilities (saving deposits), whereas for insurers the liabilities (insurance policies) typically have a much longer maturity than the assets (investments). This implies that there are netting effects between the exposures of banks and insurers. For example, if interest rates rise, this will reduce the value of the liabilities for insurers, while, for the bank, it will increase the funding cost and decrease the value of the assets.

A complicating factor in quantifying correlation or netting is the presence of embedded options in both banking and insurance products and the fact that in specific interest rate scenarios optionality will be a risk for both banks and insurance firms alike. As such, the netting effect (or correlation) might not only be unstable over time but also shows substantial different levels. An example is the prepayment option of mortgages and the yield guarantees of life insurance; both options will be exercised when interest rates are low.

To sum up, ALM provides opportunities to realise substantial diversification benefits between banking and insurance, especially when ALM risk exposures of bank and insurance firm are of similar size. For full realisation of these benefits the ALM of bank and insurance needs to be done integrally on group level to incorporate all potentials.

Credit and transfer risk

Credit risk is defined as the possible decline in value of an institution's assets due to the failure of counterparties to honour their financial obligations. Typical risk drivers are adverse changes in the business cycle and sector developments. In addition, credit risk is often reduced through the use of collateral, which in turn is dependent on certain risk drivers, for example prices of shares, bonds, commodities, commercial and residential real estate. The crux of any portfolio diversification is the way the risk drivers, for example sectors, regions, etc, are correlated with each other.

Closely related to credit risk is transfer or cross-border risk. Transfer or cross-border risk captures potential losses stemming from the possibility that funds in foreign currencies cannot be transferred out of a country as a result of action(s) by the authorities of the host country or by other events impeding the transfer. The main risk drivers are foreign exchange rates, interest rates, local business cycles and political developments. In the following, transfer risk is not addressed separately but is included as part of credit risk.

Credit risk is for most banks the main source of risk – typically approximately 50% of total economic capital – as lending activity is the main source of credit risk for most banks.[8] For a typical P&C and life insurer, however, credit risk contributes only 10–20% to total risk capital. This contribution stems mainly from investment in credit assets, for example corporate bonds.

By simply merging a bank and an insurance company one would not expect to generate substantial diversification due to credit risk as it is likely that the bank's corporate lending and the corporate bond and equity investments of the insurer are exposed to similar risk drivers.

Diversification benefits in the credit risk will not emerge with the combination of a bank and insurance firm *per se*. However, diversification benefits result if the credit risk exposure of the bank and insurer is sensitive to different risk drivers (eg, the European versus the Asian economy). Such benefits may well be material, but are not the result of combining a bank and an insurer as such. These benefits could also be obtained by merging two banks or insurers. In any case, in order to benefit systematically from diversification effects between bank and insurance credit risk exposures, active and integrated portfolio management paying active attention to the sensitivity to different risk drivers is a prerequisite.

Operational risk

The new capital adequacy framework for banks (Basel II) defines operational risk as the risk of loss resulting from inadequate or failed internal processes, people and systems or from external events. Legal risk is included in the definition; strategic and reputation risks are not (BCBS (2005)). Some insurance companies model operational risk in the same or similar way to the Basel definition. Solvency II, a future capital adequacy framework for EU insurers, has not yet given an indication on how it will deal with operational risk. [9]

Main risk drivers are the quality of control and the volume of cash flows or other business measures. For a detailed description on modelling and measuring correlation within operational risk we refer to Chapter 2.

Regardless whether it concerns banking or insurance, the challenge for operational risk is to construct reliable loss distribution models based on the still moderate data sources available. More so, as operational risk has a broad definition and thus encapsulates a wide variety of events, it also will comprise some very low-probability – but potentially very destructive – events. For such events, the high-granularity assumption used for traditional analytical models will typically not be valid and needs to be taken into account explicitly. The increase in granularity may well be the main driver of a diversification benefit between insurance and banking entities within this risk category. This benefit, however, is also likely to be present when combining multiple entities from the same industry.

Clear diversification benefits due to offsetting exposures between banking and insurance are not necessarily present as both banking and insurance are service (people) businesses with similar processes, systems, etc. Just as in the case of credit risk, diversification benefits are not based on the nature of banking or insurance business but mainly due to other business characteristics, for example cultural background or different intensity in the use of IT in different countries, which could lead to some diversification due to less-than-perfect correlation. As in the case of credit risk we conclude that diversification benefits in the operational risk area will not necessarily emerge from the combination of a bank and insurance firm.

Business risk
Business risk is the risk underlying the business a company conducts, to the extent that it includes all residual risk not covered by other risk categories such as, for instance, market/ALM, credit/transfer or operational risk. Defined more precisely, it is the exposure to loss of value due to fluctuations in volumes, margins and costs stemming from decreased demand, competitive pressure, operational efficiency, changes in regulation, etc. These fluctuations can occur because of internal, industry or wider market factors.

Here benefits are mainly dominated by diversifying the systematic risk of different businesses or strategies. For international business, the major benefit comes from diversification of national business cycles. The same argument applies in the case of different business units in different sectors (national or international) or different industries. Since banks and insurance firms still partly operate in different sectors, one would expect a diversification benefit from combining banking and insurance business in one institution as they are sensitive to different business risk drivers (eg, stock markets versus interest rates and business cycle indicators such as Gross Domestic Product (GDP)). Furthermore, this diversification benefit can be extended by the combination of strategies; for example, a market leader position in one market or country can be a good diversification with a niche position or an aggressive newcomer position in another market or country. Yet again, this is not specific for a combination of bank and insurer as such. Especially in case of diversified strategies, the quantification of diversification is an issue. A problem for the determination of diversification is that internal data series are often polluted (eg, by mergers or acquisitions) and the relevance of external data (eg, GDP national economies) for the business mix is difficult to assess.

Insurance risk

The typical core insurance risks are morbidity risk, mortality risk and P&C risk, which are defined as follows.

❑ Morbidity risk is the risk of deviations in timing and amount of cash flow (ie, claims) due to incident or non-incident of disability and sickness; risk drivers are morbidity and disability expectancy.
❑ Mortality risk is the risk of deviations in timing and amount of cash flows (premium and benefits) due to the incidence and non-incidence of death; main risk drivers are mortality and longevity expectancy.
❑ P&C risk comprises the risk of loss due to an unforeseen increase in size and frequency of claims and time-to-payment of future claims, development of outstanding claims and allocated loss adjustment expenses for P&C product lines. While it is difficult to identify specific risk drivers, changes in legislation, technology and social/economic environment impact the relative frequency and severity of claims.

Commonly, within these three risk categories, correlation between banking and insurance is irrelevant, as a bank is not normally exposed to insurance risk. Nevertheless, there can be minor indirect links between insurance risks and ALM or credit risk. For example, calamity risk that influences mortality is positively correlated with economic cycles. Of course economic cycles are also correlated with banking risks such as ALM and credit risk. Yet, this correlation is an inter-risk diversification that will be addressed in more detail in the next section.

Inter-risk diversification

The difference in exposure to various risk types between insurance and banking is likely to dominate the diversification between the two. Credit risk is the dominant risk capital at the banking side, often followed by operational and ALM risk. For insurance, it is the other way round; underwriting and market/ALM risk is of prime importance, while credit risk is of secondary interest. Consequently, the correlation coefficients used between these risks strongly affect the overall diversification benefit.

Estimating the size of the benefits from the imperfect correlation between risk types is very complex, and it is often assessed by top-down approaches in combination with simulations of correlation values. To resolve problems caused by the insufficiency of data, external indices (eg, equity prices) can be used as proxies for empirical data on the behaviour of particular risks. However, even with straightforward, simple modelling the main challenge is to get adequate data on which to base estimates of inter-risk correlation.

It is intuitively clear that diversification between risk types is very much dependent on the context in which the bank and the insurer operate. Some general patterns in correlation between risk types seem to exist. For instance, in the case of the combination of credit and ALM (and market) risk it is mostly assumed to that both risks will move together in extreme situations. However, for interest rate risk (which is the dominating ALM risk in banks), the opposite holds: interest (mismatch) income typically increases when credit losses increase, due to lower (short-term) interest rates and steeper yield curves in bad economic times.

The correlation between market, credit and/or business risk may be relatively high as all of these risks are primarily dominated by economic and financial developments. An example would be that in a bear equity market ("market risk") commission income tends to be reduced ("business risk").

The combination of operational risk with the other risk categories may well result in higher diversification benefits. One could argue that the risk of fraud or technical failures of systems is not at all correlated with the movements of interest rates (market risk) or the probability of default (credit risk) of a mortgage, for instance. However, there might be a low correlation between operational risks and other risks due to an indirect linkage by general economic circumstances. In times of an economic downturn, credit risk is high and cost cutting may take place. Tight budgets might lead to keeping older (riskier) systems in operation for longer than is prudent. Moreover, operational risk losses often only become apparent when credit or market losses occur as only then will errors in documentation, eg, become apparent.

A similar argument holds for a relatively low correlation of insurance risk with the other risk types; for example, morbidity risk is not correlated with currency risk (market risk) but calamity risk will be weakly correlated with financial markets.

Empirical estimates

The materiality of diversification can be determined in a number of ways, on a consolidated basis or using granular data. In the former approach, data on a high level of aggregation are combined to see whether banking and insurance undertakings are similar or not. In the latter approach, granular data on individual risk types are aggregated using assumptions on correlations. This approach is more in line with the approach chosen in this book. To cover both approaches, however, we will first summarise the findings of the consolidated approach.

The literature on diversification effects across sectors is fed by the primarily American discussion as to what activities are permitted for bank holding companies (BHSs).[10] The relative impact of mixing banking activities with various other kinds of activities has been discussed in depth and this discussion is nested in the more general debate on whether diversification is always a good thing for any company, to which the answer is often thought to be negative (cf, Berger and Ofek 1995; Lamont and Polk 2002).

Research can be categorised into studies that look at activities already permitted (Wall 1987) and at "forbidden" activities (Boyd *et al* 1993).[11] Another distinction that can be drawn is between studies using market information and studies using book values (eg, Estrella 2001) compared with the work of Boyd and Graham. There is some debate as to whether accounting or market data provide the best measure of risk and return. It is well known that accounting data show a smoothed picture of profits, partly because assets and liabilities are shown at historical cost rather than at market value. Stock prices, in contrast, quickly reflect all relevant information as it becomes known. However, equity price series show substantial volatility indicating that factors other than just the developments relevant to the value of the firm itself are reflected. Some of the studies on hypothetical mergers have been criticised because the variability of profits has been used instead of the more appropriate probability of bankruptcy (Santos 1998). Other studies use measures aggregated over industries, introducing an aggregation bias. Finally, it has been pointed out that a merger is more than just combining balance sheets. Following a merger, policies are very likely to be changed to take advantage of the new situation. The conclusions reached are mixed. Life insurance seems to be unambiguously a good choice for banks

looking for a reduction of risk. <u>Diversification into real estate seems</u>
<u>to generally increase risk but the strength of this result might be dri-</u>
<u>ven by particular sample selections</u>. The effect of diversification into
securities activities seems to be unclear, depending on method,
period or definition. There are relatively few studies using European
data (see, eg, Gully *et al* 2001; Bikker and Van Lelyveld 2003;
Slijkerman *et al* 2005). The study by Bikker and Van Lelyveld (2003)
shows that substantial diversification effects exist but that they are
not necessarily achieved by merging across sectors. The recent study
by Slijkerman *et al* (2005) looks at tail correlation of banking and
insurance equity returns and finds that the largest diversification
effects in extreme circumstances are found in mergers across sectors.

Having discussed the consolidated approach we can now turn to
a more granular approach. As will be clear by now, the materiality
of diversification effects depend very much on the portfolio of the
particular institution, the way and up to which level risks are
aggregated or the presence of netting effects. These difficulties are
reflected in the limited number of firms that have published economic capital numbers with and without diversification effects,
and the subsequent difficulties in interpreting the range of the
numbers. Berg-Yuen and Medova (2004) have made a valiant
attempt to collect published economic capital numbers and these
are reported in Table 7.

Table 7 shows that diversification effects range from a low of
7.2% to a high of 33.49%. Such a range is the result of both differences in the underlying risk profile but are also the result of different measurement and aggregation methodologies. In more detail,
Dimakos and Aas (2003) provide an estimate for Den Norske Bank,
a Norwegian bank, and find a very conservative estimate already
yields a diversification benefit of 20% in total economic capital over
a one-year horizon.

Using variability in earnings as a measure of bank risk Kuritzkes
and Schuermann (2006) take data from over 300 US bank holding
companies with total assets of at least $1bn over the last two
decades. Based on their analysis, Kuritzkes and Schuermann conclude that diversification benefits lie between 31% and 47%. This is
in line with earlier results of Rosenberg and Schuermann (2006),
although the latter authors use copula's to arrive at their conclusions. The estimated correlations between risks, as estimated by

Table 7 Diversification effect as a percentage of economic capital (in 2002 and 2003)

Institution	2002	2003
Citigroup	–	10.02
Deutsche Bank	–	7.20
JP Morgan Chase	18.77	12.38
Credit Suisse	54.44	33.49
Commerzbank	–	21.78
Dresdner Bank	–	22.64
Dexia	18.25	15.00

Source: Berg-Yuen and Medova (2004, Table 5.9, p 28).

Kuritzkes and Schuermann (2006), re relatively small and some-times even negative.

However, as Berben and Jansen (2005) have shown recently, the correlation of bond and stock returns among European countries and the U.S. has been positive and has increased substantially over the last 20 years (from 0.2 in 1980s to 0.9 in 2003 for bond returns and from 0.2 to 0.7 for stock returns). For a financial institution, active in both continents in equal proportions, such an increase in correlation would imply a drop in diversification benefits from of 11% (15%) percent for bonds (stocks). Taken together it is clear that selecting and estimating the relevant parameters should not be taken too lightly. Depending on the activities of the financial insti-tutions, the relevant parameters should be selected and then esti-mated. These estimates might differ significantly from the number mentioned in this paragraph.

Turning to insurance companies, another source for information on the size of diversification effects is a study published by the Chief Risk Officer Forum (CRO (2005)). In this study, a sample of 11 large insurance companies is analysed. The study shows that diver-sification benefits range from 30% to 60% with a median value of 51%. These numbers are thus more or less in line with those found in the banking industry.

As noted earlier, interpreting diversification outcomes is extremely difficult. For instance, we roughly estimated (in the "Correlation, net-ting and granularity" section) that the diversification benefit of two financial units with economic capital of even size and uncorrelated risk would probably not exceed 30%. Presuming that negative correlation of risk drivers under extreme events (economic capital) are rarely found, diversification benefits above 30% are only possible if netting effects are present or if more aggregation levels (eg, units and inter-risk) are included in determining the benefit. For a thorough interpretation of the reported diversification benefits an outsider still needs a lot more additional information, for example a basic aggregation model, netting effects or stand-alone size of risk capitals.

ALLOCATION
Once diversification is properly taken in to account, total economic capital will be lower than the stand-alone economic capital amounts of the business units. A question is whether to allocate the diversification benefits to the business units, or not. If diversification benefits are not handed down to the business units, each unit is expected to operate on a stand-alone basis. The "optimal" level of group risk-taking can be achieved only when diversification benefits are allocated to business units. That is, it is preferable for each business unit to be assigned an economic capital allocation closer to its contribution to the total economic capital amount, as opposed to what its economic capital requirement would be on a stand-alone basis.

For investment decisions, an assessment of diversification on a marginal basis is relevant, since this determines the marginal costs associated with the investment. This forms the lower boundary in the determination of a minimum required return. For performance management, ie, the best incentives for efficient capital use, diversification benefits should be allocated completely to the business units. Allocation of diversification benefits, however, complicates performance management, as diversification effects are difficult to manage for a business unit within a conglomerate.

Proper allocation should produce the right incentives ("less risk, less capital") and prevent capital arbitrage within the economic capital framework. For example, no portfolio should undercut the proposed allocation: an undercut occurs when a portfolio's allocation is higher than the stand-alone economic capital. The rationale is that the portfolio cannot justifiably be allocated more risk capital than it can possibly have brought to the firm.

Furthermore, allocation should be consistent with the risk measure used. For example, if risk is measured using standard deviation, then the risk allocation should be based on the contribution to the standard deviation. Alternatively, if risk is measured using VAR, then the risk allocation should be based on the contribution to the VAR. Different risk measures will imply different risk contributions to the total risk for a particular unit.

Taking all these considerations together, three possible methods of allocating diversification benefits can be discerned.[12]

1. *No allocation* of benefits to business units. In this case, all benefits are held at the corporate level.
2. *Allocation on a pro-rata basis* using some weighting scheme (eg, reserves or earnings).
3. *Allocate capital using the marginal approach.* This method can be split into a discrete and a continuous marginal approach.
   a. In the discrete approach, the change in economic capital is calculated if a particular business unit is removed from the calculations. The absolute value of this amount is subsequently allocated to the particular business unit. The remainder of

Table 8 Comparison of economic capital allocation mechanisms.

Method	In favour	Against
No allocation	❏ Simple ❏ Business units should only receive benefits for risk that it can control as allocation is outside their control it only adds volatility to their capital	❏ Could lead to over-investment ❏ No incentive to hedge risk concentrations at corporate level ❏ Impact of corporate strategy changes is hardly captured
Marginal approach	❏ Allocates true economic capital ❏ Allows units to fully benefit from being part of the group (diversification), ie, pricing and growth potential ❏ Reflects concentrations in overall risk profile	❏ Complicated
Pro-rata	❏ Simple ❏ Capital allocation is not to business units	❏ Allocates capital linked to risk contribution of the business unit

capital, after capital is allocated to all the subsidiaries, is allocated to the corporate (holding) level.

b. In the continuous case, capital is allocated to a unit proportionally to its contribution to the overall risk profile. This approach ensures that, in case no risk is taken at corporate level, all capital is allocated to the risk-taking business units. Furthermore, it is consistent with portfolio theory and as such ensures that possible concentrations are reflected. Therefore, the arguments in favour of allocation are the strongest in this approach.

Each of these approaches has both arguments in favour and against as summarised in Table 8.

DATA QUALITY AND MIS-ESTIMATION

It has been mentioned several times that a crucial issue for estimating diversification benefits is *data quality*. Adequate and sufficient representative data is necessary to have correct information on possible correlation of specific risk drivers.

In general two types of data problems can be identified.

1. Lack of data, for instance involving operational risk. This makes it difficult to assess the risks, especially in the tails of the risk distribution.
2. Inconsistency of data. This plays an important role when one aggregates risk positions and/or economic capital amounts to higher levels. The data used to calculate economic capital for the bank should be consistent with the data used within the insurance firm(s) to estimate capital. Thus, for instance, the definition of default for mortgages used to determine credit risk capital should be the same.

To make matters even more complex, a trade-off between the two problems exists. If data is generally collected at a very low and detailed level at all units, data consistency can be addressed in a relatively straightforward manner, as one can always drill down to the lowest data level. Then, if necessary, data information can be restructured to meet the desired definition before aggregating to higher levels. However, a detailed level of data information will probably result in missing data on tail events for many data categories. Thus, the modelling of the risk distribution is likely to be inaccurate.

Furthermore, optimal data quality at the lowest level, making modelling possible, would require extensive information for a complete description of all risk drivers. Such a level of detail would be inefficient, as it would demand a prohibitive workload from the organisation. Yet, simple high-level data will definitely miss some crucial economic links on the lower level and lead to economically suboptimal decisions. In fact, each management layer has to find an optimal balance with regard to this trade-off for data gathering; on the one hand too high a level of data is undesirable due to consistency problems and on the other hand too low a level of data means data gets scarce and the workload increases.

Closely related to the data quality issue is the problem of *mis-estimation* of models resulting in an over- or underestimation of diversification. Here the previously mentioned concentration and granularity issues come to the fore again. In particular, due to the data problems and necessary simplifications it is clear that estimates of diversification are likely to be imprecise. In any case one should try to assess the effect of this possible estimation error in order to assure that it is relatively small.

REGULATORY CONSIDERATIONS

Diversification effects can currently be modelled in many ways and no dominant best practice with respect to modelling diversification has as yet emerged in the industry. From the supervisory point of view, the lack of comprehensive risk models is an issue. If models are incomplete, ie, not all risk factors included, this could result in an underestimation of correlation and consequently to an overestimation of diversification benefits. Given the uncertainties around present modelling, it is important to check the model for robustness (ie, for sensitivity of model parameters). Also by back-testing the model, one could get more insight into the properties of various model choices.[13]

An additional supervisory concern is the plausibility of the model in times of (market) stress. Parameter values might change under stressed conditions (eg, correlation). Moreover, especially in times of stress, the underlying assumption of correlation estimates becomes strained. Most modelling assumes that there is a linear relation between risks. If the empirical relation is non-linear, the correlation may be underestimated and consequently the diversification benefits will be overestimated.

An additional issue for internationally active financial institutions is that diversification benefits have to be acknowledged in numerous jurisdictions. This implies that the institution and all supervisors concerned will have to agree on the acceptable method and outcome. Such a consensus should be actively pursued to avoid duplication of "validation" of economic capital models. However, even if a consensus is reached about the appropriate method and amount of aggregate economic capital, host supervisors might require stand-alone capitalisation of subsidiaries in their jurisdiction. In case that diversification was fully taken in to account in the aggregate economic capital and has been allocated to the business unit, this might imply that some other part of the conglomerate would be undercapitalised. From a supervisory perspective, in such situations a trade-off between multiple supervisory goals exists. On the one hand, supervisors need to create the right incentives for the supervised institutions, which is an argument in favour of the allocation of diversification benefits. On the other hand, legal restrictions, and in particular restrictions on the international "mobility" of capital within a financial institution in combination with the existence of consumer protections schemes, gives the supervisor less leeway than would be desirable from an economic perspective.

Authors of this chapter:
Hugo Everts, ING Group and Hartwig Liersch, ING Group.

1   In the present discussion we will concentrate on the determination of economically (as opposed to regulatory) required capital and abstracts from issues regarding the exact definition and eligibility of different buffers and its interaction with accounting treatment (ie, the definition of capital discussion).

2   If one institution has 1.000 risk positions, each of which may result in a loss of €10 and another institution has 1.000 risk positions and 999 carry a risk of €1 whereas its last position carries a risk of €9.001, both have 1.000 counterparties and both have a total risk position of €10.000. However, the second institution's risk will be much larger than the first institution's risk, since its effective number of risk positions is rather small.

3   More precisely, for multiple risk components: you need to pre- and post-multiply the correlation matrix with the vector of separate risk capitals per risk type, and subsequently take the square root. In other words, $EC = \sqrt{x^T \Sigma x}$, with Σ the correlation matrix and x the vector of stand-alone risk capitals per risk driver.

4 Although the size of the correlation matrix can reach an impressive size: with four positions, each can be compared with the three other positions for a total of 12 combinations (Nuxoll 1999). Eliminating duplicate observations (the correlations between x and y is the same as between y and x) and the diagonal of 1 (correlation of x with itself), we are left with six possible pairs. With 100 positions the possible number of unique pairs is already 4,950.

5 For a more detailed and formalised explanation of dependency and copulas see Groupe Consultatif (2005) or Embrechts *et al* (2002).

6 Adapted from Saita (2004).

7 Here a high, positive effect (see the "Correlation, netting and granularity" section). As such, netting effects are sometimes captured as a "negative correlation" in case a financial institution uses a correlation based approach for risk aggregation.

8 See disclosures, for example annual reports, of several bank/insurers such as Citigroup, Rabobank, JP Morgan Chase, Deutsche Bank, Barclays, Fortis, Nordea, ING Bank, Fortis and Allianz (& Dresdner).

9 Solvency II, a future capital adequacy framework for insurers, has not yet given an indication on how it will deal with operational risk.

10 This section is based on Bikker and Van Lelyveld (2003). The debate was especially relevant in the abolition of the Glass-Steagall act (see Kwan and Laderman 1999). The BHC literature is discussed in Laderman (2000). For additional information see Boyd and Graham (1988), Boyd *et al* (1993), Estrella (2001), Gully *et al* (2001), Kwan and Laderman (1999), Kwast (1989), Lown *et al* (2000) and Santomero and Chung (1992).

11 See Boyd *et al* (1993) for an overview of many of the relevant papers.

12 Compare with Joint Forum (2003) and Societies of Actuaries (2004, pp 38–39). For a more technical discussion, see Koyluoglu and Stoker (2002).

13 In aggregating all risks in a comprehensive manner the institution may in principle take into account correlation between risk types under the so-called Pillar II approach to capital adequacy; see Compendium paper (Committee of European Banking Supervisors (CEBS) (2004, p 10)), published by the CEBS, 24th May 2004.

5

A Survey of Economic Capital Model Implementation

Iman van Lelyveld, Moncef Boughanmi, Henk van Broekhoven, Hugo Everts, Maarten Gelderman, Olav Jones, Pieter Klaassen, Hartwig Liersch, Raymond Monnik, André Pouw, Gaston Siegelaer, Henrico Wanders

This chapter presents an overview of the current state of risk modelling in a selected number of internationally active financial conglomerates. The chapter is a natural extension of the description of economic capital methodology in the previous chapters, giving a comprehensive view of concepts and best practice in economic capital modelling. Here we survey the present state-of-play in implementation at the number of institutions that are at the forefront of implementing economic capital models. In particular, we have incorporated the experiences of ABN AMRO, Fortis, ING Group and Rabobank. Wherever applicable, we extend our survey with (public) information about implementation at other internationally active institutions.

In the description of the current state-of-play it will become clear that, in many areas (model) implementation is not in steady state but is undergoing rapid change. An important, external influence in this process is the approaching implementation of the new supervisory frameworks Basel II and Solvency II for the banking and insurance sectors, respectively. Given the timelines of both projects and scarce resources, institutions have understandably chosen to focus on first improving models on the banking side. A similar acceleration of activities can be expected on the insurance side as the Solvency II framework becomes more solid.

The survey has uncovered a wealth of information about the current state of implementation of economic capital models at large Dutch financial conglomerates and revealed a number of commonalities. All participating institutions have a model in place producing an economic capital amount estimated to be sufficient to cover ULs at some pre-defined confidence level. These models are for instance used for capital allocation, performance measurement and external reporting although the importance of each of these purposes differs by institution.

Another commonality is that institutions have conceptually consistent models for each risk type across sectors, although practical considerations might lead to slightly different implementation in parts of the conglomerate. An example of the common conceptual framework is the implementation of market risk VAR models. These models have a relatively long history on the banking side but have a short time-horizon, due to their risk management origins and the relatively short holding period of trading positions. Thus, on the banking side, to come to an estimate of the annual VAR, the short-term VAR numbers are scaled up. On the insurance side, legacy models are less of an issue and thus the models for market risk tend to be capable of computing annual VAR numbers directly.

In ranking the relative reliability of models, there seems to be a consensus on the banking side; market risk is placed first, followed by credit, operational and business risk. On the insurance side, more divergent views prevail; for instance, for market, credit and insurance risk all three risk types are chosen as the most reliable model at least once.

INTRODUCTION

This chapter gives an overview of the current state of risk modelling in Dutch financial conglomerates. The overview in this chapter builds on the description of economic capital methodology in the previous three chapters. In particular, in the second chapter we presented a classification of risks and risk drivers that we employed in our subsequent discussion of the appropriate approach in economic capital modelling. Then, in Chapter 3 we turned our attention to risk measures, the time horizon and the valuation principles to be used in economic capital models. Finally, in the previous chapter, we discussed the handling of diversification and aggregation of risk measures. Together, these three chapters give a comprehensive view of concepts and best practice in economic capital modelling. Now, we will survey the present state-of-play in implementation at the participating institutions: ABN AMRO, Fortis, ING Group and Rabobank.

A common factor between the participating institutions is that they view risk as a key strategic issue; satisfying stakeholders' needs is more risky today than in the past. Implementing an integrated strategic risk management approach allows firms to consistently deliver superior performance while pro-actively managing risk. There is a need for a holistic approach, however, and in implementing such an approach each institution has made different choices, driven by for instance by firm specific legacy systems. It is therefore very difficult to provide a one-size-fits-all blueprint although many outlines exist (see for instance Clark and Varma 1999). According to these authors we could broadly speaking discern the following steps:

1. *Set direction.* In this stage the significant risks are identified. Areas of critical concern are discussed and priorities are set.
2. *Baseline and benchmark.* The major risks are quantified. This naturally implies making assumptions but, at the same time, it makes gaps in measurement and understanding apparent.
3. *Create the vision.* A risk management vision is created comprising three key components of measuring, managing and monitoring risk. Subsequently, an appropriate strategy may be developed.
4. *Design process improvements.* Based on the insights in the previous steps, current systems might be improved or new systems designed.
5. *Implement Change.* The updates are implemented and the new systems are put in place.
6. *Embed continuous improvements.* Implementing risk management systems is not a once-off activity. As the overall framework becomes well embedded, it becomes increasingly more important to identify and implement incremental improvements.

Within an implementation process, four stages of development can be discerned. First there is an *entrepreneurial stage*. In this stage, the approach is ad hoc and well defined procedures have yet to emerge. The second stage could be termed *bureaucracy*. Formal procedures are defined in this stage. Deliverables and responsibilities are defined and assigned. In the third stage the focus is on *process management*: processes are improved, some functions or teams are empowered, risk management is separated from commercial functions with their focus on shareholder value creation. A final stage could be the *strategic risk management stage*. In this stage risk management would (ideally) be integrated with shareholder value-based management.

The main focus of the present paper is describing the current state-of-play. However, in many areas we will cover, (model) implementation is not in a steady state but is undergoing rapid change. An important, external influence in this process is the upcoming implementation of new supervisory frameworks Basel II and Solvency II for the banking and insurance sectors, respectively. Given the timelines of both projects and scarce resources, institutions have understandably chosen to focus on improving models on the banking side first. As Solvency II becomes more solid and implementation nears, a similar speeding up of activities can be expected on the insurance side.

Another issue we will also pay attention to is validation. Although limited data availability might make rigorous statistical backtesting unfeasible, the model's users naturally would like to attain a certain level of comfort in the sense that the model gives a good account of an institution's present and future capital needs. In discussing these issues, we will cover both the methods applied and the organisational structures in place.

The structure of this chapter is as follows. First, we will briefly mention other publications that provide overviews of the state of economic capital modelling. Then we will turn to the stated objectives of economic capital models followed by a brief review of the overall coverage. This is followed by a number of introductory remarks concerning, amongst others, time horizon, organisational setting and reliability. Then we will discuss each of the risk types in turn followed by some remarks on future developments. Finally, we conclude.

PREVIOUS SURVEYS

As the subject of economic capital has attracted considerable attention in recent years, a number of surveys have been undertaken recently to document current practice. Some surveys have been undertaken by consultants. An example of such an approach is the PWC (2004) survey. Others have been undertaken by practitioners such as the Chief Risk Officers Forum, for instance, or professional bodies such as the Economic Capital subgroup of the Societies of Actuaries Risk Management Task Force (Societies of Actuaries 2004) and by a UK group of actuaries (UK Working Party 2003).[1]

OBJECTIVES FOR ECONOMIC CAPITAL MODELS

Economic capital models can serve a number of purposes, which we will discuss in turn. At present, economic capital is mainly determined for internal use. Outcomes are, for instance, used to allocate capital across business units or to evaluate the performance of staff. For more senior staff in particular this information might feed more or less directly in to the determination of performance related pay. In addition, economic capital models are in some cases used as input for (risk-based) pricing or limit setting. Occasionally, economic capital models are used to determine possible diversification benefits in (prospective) takeover candidates. An external use of economic capital models is in communicating with stakeholders: all participating institutions mention economic capital outcomes in external reporting (ie, annual reports) in varying detail. In the future, the model outcomes might be used to determine the amount of economic capital for regulatory solvency.

All of the abovementioned objectives are important for all of the institutions participating in our survey, although to a different degree. All institutions use their economic capital model to determine capital for risk management purposes. In this process model, outcomes are compared with available capital. In addition, the model outcomes are used in the allocation of capital (ie, risk limits for individual obligors and/or sectors) and (as an input for) pricing.

With regard to the use of the model for evaluating the performance, and consequently, determination of performance related pay, the picture is more diverse. All institutions use the model in some way to evaluate performance on a more or less aggregated level (business units). In addition, the performance related pay of the higher echelons of management is in some cases partly determined using economic capital outcomes. The economic capital outcomes are thus at present not used directly for performance related pay at lower levels in the organisation. However, if economic capital models are used at higher levels, then personnel at lower levels will be influenced, at least indirectly. Moreover, participating institutions see a continued trend towards further, more granular use of economic capital in this respect.

IMPLEMENTATION OF ECONOMIC CAPITAL MODELS: AN OVERVIEW

Institutions generally discern the various risk types as given in the second chapter, ie, Market/ALM, Credit (including transfer or country risk), Life, P&C or non-life, Operational and Business or Strategic risk. Furthermore, institutions use the inputs and models as given in our earlier taxonomy. We will now first give a general overview of implementation for all risk types. This will be followed in the next section by remarks relevant to all risk types followed by some more detailed remarks for each of the discerned risk types.

For market or ALM risk, all institutions use VAR models for banking and, if applicable, in insurance. These models are generally at book level. In addition, stress tests or Monte Carlo scenarios are used as supplementary analysis. The models are not necessarily identical across sectors although harmonisation within ALM is intended to take place in the future.

Currently, relatively sophisticated credit risk models are in place or are to be implemented shortly on the banking side. Most new models are consistent with the Basel II guideline and involve separate estimates of the probability of default (PD), the loss given default (LGD), exposure at default (EAD) and maturity. Some institutions use approximations for some portfolios; ULs are for instance assumed to be some multiple of expected loss (EL). To calculate economic capital, correlation within portfolios or correlations with risk drivers are used. Together, this information leads to economic capital amounts. The availability of the inputs to internal credit models make it relatively easy to implement the Internal Ratings Based (IRB) approaches under Basel II since they rely on the same parameters.

For the insurance side, credit risk has historically been less of an issue and the models have thus evolved less. However, in most cases model development and implementation is underway. An advantage in this area is that models developed on the banking side can be adapted for insurance with relatively little effort. This implies that, also with respect to the integrated model (full) harmonisation is approaching. Cross-border credit risk, ie, transfer or country risk, is sometimes modelled separately involving parameters such as PD, LGD and EAD but this is not the case for all institutions.

In the measurement of life insurance risks there seems to be a reasonable level of consensus. Moreover, for both mortality and for morbidity or disability, the same approach is taken. All institutions use assessments of the surplus and some form of stress testing or other measures of resilience for both determining economic capital and validation. Such a stress test could for instance be the application of a shock to the mortality table used on the current portfolio. For P&C or non-life, all institutions use similar approaches as well, although implementation will differ. For extreme events (catastrophe risk), exceedence probability curves are employed while in the case of non-catastrophe P&C, frequency based severity modelling, loss triangle analysis and historical claim ratios are also used, again for economic capital determination and validation.

It is clear that the measurement of operational risk is an area in rapid development. Most institutions, however, already have a model in place or are in the middle of development on the banking side. If operational risk is also modelled on the insurance side, then the same model is used for both sectors. These models all employ historical loss data over quite a number of years (up to 25 years). In some cases, a scorecard approach is used to measure the quality of control(s) in a business line. The information gained through scorecards is used by some institutions to fine-tune economic capital allocation.

In business or strategic risk, all institutions analyse historical earnings volatility. Generally, this volatility is cleansed for the influence of other risks (ie, market, credit and operational risk). For lapse risk and expense risk, which are also included under this header, more extensive analyses are performed. In some cases, aspects of these insurance side approaches will be extended to the banking side.

ECONOMIC CAPITAL FOR LESS SOPHISTICATED INSTITUTIONS

Implementing an economic capital concept in an institution is a long and costly process. In a recent survey of 44 large insurers (PWC 2004), 43% of the respondents indicate that this time taken to develop an economic capital model lies between three and five years. For smaller institutions, the timeline will probably be shorter but many smaller institutions, overawed by highly complex economic capital models, feel that implementing an economic capital model is not feasible. This section argues that smaller, less sophisticated institutions could also build suitable models.

After securing senior management commitment, the main issue is the availability and collection of sufficient high-quality data that is required to develop and maintain the various risk models.[2] In addition, the required infrastructure tends to be complex and generally requires substantial investments. Although the data and infrastructure requirements can form sizable hurdles, securing and maintaining senior management commitment is likely to be a more important issue than these two technical issues combined, as the potential impact on the existing business and organisation can be very large.

The first step in implementing an economic capital model would be the identification of existing risk types in the organisation or, in other words, the creation of a risk map. This is required to ensure that all risks will be covered by the economic capital concept. For each risk type, an assessment of the available risk management tools has to be made. This ranges from measuring (ie, what models are available) to monitoring and reporting and thus has to include all available models, data, infrastructure, etc.

The next step will be to leverage off the existing tools and use what is available to make the first top-down calculations for economic capital. Although these calculations will be imprecise they are invaluable in the sense that imprecision will make clear where to first improve measurement (and then management). The easiest risk types to deal with tend to be market and interest rate risk. For banking, the coverage and reporting of these risk types has already been required for several years under Basel I. The new credit risk concepts are more sophisticated and might not yet be in operation. Operational risk and business risk generally are not yet covered at all.

A good guideline in this respect may be provided by the Basel II document. Although Basel II does not recognise important aspects such as diversification effects, the models can serve as a proxy for the economic capital framework. It is very important, however, to understand what the exact differences between Basel II and a sophisticated economic capital framework are. As smaller institutions tend to be more concentrated, management might want to adapt the Basel II models in order to capture granularity and credit risk concentration issues. This is where the availability and collection of good quality data becomes important. In the areas where data is an issue, external benchmarks may have to be used to make the models work. Benchmarks or peer experience can for instance be obtained from the many conferences that are held on economic capital and related issues.

It is important to recognise that weak measurement needs to be compensated by good management. Putting the proper policies and procedures in place may not improve the calculations, but is an important step towards understanding the key elements of the various risk types and their effects on business.

Ultimately, the top-down calculations will have to be replaced by bottom-up figures. To what extent a bank will be successful in this transition will again largely depend on the quality and availability of sufficient data. For several risk types, collecting sufficient data can be infeasible (eg, credit risk resulting from sovereign defaults) and thus understanding the key elements and being able to build an "expert-based" model around it may turn out to be an acceptable solution. For other risk types, data is available but only in hard copy files and data entry might be prohibitively costly.

As economic capital models are generally made to measure, a significant part of the costs of an economic capital model is more or less fixed. For smaller institutions these fixed cost will thus be an important factor for any decision on the implementation of an economic capital framework. Given the data and other issues that surround the more sophisticated economic capital models, it might be appropriate to use the Basel II Standardised Approach as a basis for the economic capital model. For risks, not prescribed in the first pillar (eg, interest rate risk in the banking book) own solutions should be found. For insurance undertakings, the regulatory requirements emerging from the Solvency process can be a source of inspiration.

The Basel Standardised Approach is easy to adapt and if an institution wants to calibrate its capital to a level other than Basel's 99.5% it can easily accomplish this, as the underlying implicit assumption is a normal distribution. The implicitly assumed portfolio invariance and the adding up characteristic of the Standardised Approach make the capital allocation, performance measurement and pricing simple and easy. The complication of correlations and diversification effects are assumed away. The simplicity of this framework has its drawbacks, as it does not capture the true risk of the portfolio. This can be interpreted as a trade-off between costs and model precision.

GENERAL REMARKS ABOUT ALL RISK TYPES
Introduction
In the second chapter we proposed a taxonomy of the various risks. This classification will be used as a framework to discuss the present state of implementation of economic capital models in Dutch financial conglomerates. First we will discuss a number of general issues that are relevant for all risk types. The issues that we will discuss in turn are: (1) time horizon and confidence level, (2) aggregation, (3) validation methods, (4) commercial interests, development and the organisation of internal validation, (5) data availability, and, finally, (6) model reliability. Then we will cover a number of issues for each risk type: management action, assumptions, information on performance and risk drivers, use of external data, inclusion of risk self-assessment, consistency and, finally, validation. In some cases repetition is unfortunately unavoidable because similar approaches are followed for two or more risks or in case issues are applicable to all risk types.

Time horizon and confidence level
All institutions use a time horizon of one year. Confidence levels are chosen to reflect target ratings and range from 99.95% to 99.99%. The correspondence between the target rating and the confidence level depends on – amongst others – the internal definition of capital and the calibration method. Please note that a VAR of 99.00%, for instance, does not result in the same level of comfort as a Tail VAR of 99.00%. This target range is consistent with the range of chosen confidence intervals reported in Berg-Yuen and Medova (2004, p 24), running up from 99.00% to 99.98%. Credit Suisse is a clear outlier here with "only" a 99.00% confidence level. In contrast, in a survey of insurance companies and consultants, conducted under the auspices of the Society of Actuaries (Societies of Actuaries 2004), a much wider range of confidence intervals applied are reported. Interestingly, some institutions use unexpected values. The distribution of confidence levels reported is shown in Figure 10.

The time horizon and the confidence levels are the same across sectors within each institution. For market risk on the banking side, the shorter time horizon VARs are extrapolated to an annual figure at the desired confidence level. These short-term measures might

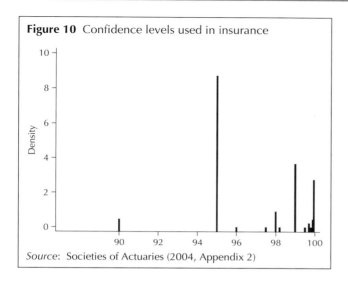

Figure 10 Confidence levels used in insurance

Source: Societies of Actuaries (2004, Appendix 2)

be computed at a different (lower) confidence level. On the insurance side, such scaling up is less prevalent because, in contrast with the banking side, models had to be implemented from scratch. This allowed institutions to build in such functionality relatively easily since development was not hindered by legacy systems. For business risk, the confidence level is in some cases implicit; the stress tests used are deemed to match some chosen confidence level.

Aggregation

As discussed in the chapter on diversification and aggregation there are generally two approaches to calculate economic capital. In the first approach, economic capital is first calculated per risk type for the institution as a whole, and subsequently the economic capital results per risk type are aggregated to an overall economic capital estimate. In the second approach, economic capital is first calculated for individual business units (comprising all relevant risk types), and then the economic capital results per business unit are aggregated to an overall economic capital estimate. Most institutions use the first approach (per risk type first, then combine) in banking while the second approach (per business unit first for all risks, then combine) is implemented on the insurance side. The overall approach is thus a mixture of the two approaches.

An issue that is related to the previous practical choice(s) is the question of whether models are consistent for each risk type across the institution or, alternatively, whether they are only consistent within business units. Generally, approaches are consistent within the banking and insurance sectors. Furthermore, the approach towards market, credit and operational risk is generally conceptually consistent across both sectors. Differences might occur with regard to measurement approaches and/or reporting requirements.

Another important aspect in (sub)aggregation is the mix between more and less advanced approaches. Generally, for credit and market risk a fine-grained approach is in use. Diversification effects on the aggregate are in some cases passed on to lower business units. For operational risk and business risk, some institutions use individual data as well. Other institutions, however, use a more broad-brush approach. For such an approach, the required capital for the particular risk type is first determined at the top level and then allocated to the organisational units below.

In aggregating, generally some variant of the variance–covariance method is in use. In this method a matrix with all the correlation values between all the risks in the institution should – at least theoretically – be available. In practice, all institutions use assumptions and in making these assumptions, institutions tend to build in some prudence. Some institutions recognise diversification but limit its effects by allowing correlation within business units for a single risk but not across business units. Assumptions with somewhat more impact, used by some institutions, are to assume that risk types are perfectly correlated (ie, no diversification) or, on the contrary, that some risk types have low correlation with other risk types (eg, operational risk and the other risk types). Note that, regardless of the exact assumptions made, netting (ie, offsetting exposures) can still take place.

Validation methods

Various methods are employed to validate models. The most important of these are backtesting, scenario analysis and benchmarking. Backtesting is the comparison of model results with historical realisations. Scenario analysis entails the definition of a set of movements of risk drivers, possibly including developments over time. The cohesion in the parameter movements is provided by historical or hypothetical developments (eg, a recession or severe slump in property prices). Given this state of the world, the effects on the institutions current position are computed. In coming up with plausible scenarios, some institutions employ methodology platforms, bringing together experts. The resulting scenarios are generally a mix of both historical and hypothetical experiences. Stress testing is a simpler variation in the sense that only the extreme movement in the risk driver is defined (arbitrarily) and that this shock does not have to form part of a coherent whole. The dividing line between stress testing and scenario analysis is, however, not a clear-cut division. Benchmarking generally takes on two forms. First, it can entail a comparison with peers. Second, it can be a comparison with industry standards (ie, vendor models). The outcomes of the validation exercises are, in some institutions, used explicitly as a part of the economic capital calculations. Other institutions use these exercises primarily to test the robustness of the economic model.

Commercial interests, development and validation

An important issue in both development and validation of economic capital models is the proper balance between the influence of the commercial functions on the one hand, and those responsible for building and assessing the validity of the models, on the other. Institutions have chosen different approaches to resolving this issue. One possibility to curtail interference from commercial interests in developing economic capital models is to place the responsibility for development completely outside the commercial business units. However, to assure that the model remains realistic, commercial business units should be able to challenge economic capital methodologies. Thus, some institutions have significant involvement of commercial functions in the development of their model. In addition, once agreement is reached, the methodology is approved in senior risk committees and/or by senior risk management. *Ex post* validation can either be allocated to the risk management function or to independent corporate audit departments, although these audit departments tend to focus on evaluating the process rather than the model.

Data availability

Institutions have a wealth of data at their disposal but their practical use is more apparent than real. One reason is that much of the information is only available in dispersed, physical dossiers. Converting this data into usable information can then be prohibitively costly. A second reason is that although credit histories might go back quite some time, they generally do not include a number of relevant parameters; eg, periodic estimates of the PD for a specific credit, using a definition (broadly) consistent with the presently used definition, are not likely to be included.

Reliability

Given the available data, approaches differ in whether it is primarily a bottom-up or a top-down approach. A bottom-up approach is defined as an approach where there is a relative wealth of information at a disaggregated level while a top-down approach uses aggregated data to determine the level of economic capital that is then allocated downward. For most risk types, the approach chosen is a mixture of the two. However, the emphasis for market and credit risk is on the bottom-up side while aggregated data plays a much more important role for operational risk and business risk.

The models for the various risk types have different levels of sophistication because of materiality or of data availability. The lack of materiality of some risks can lead institutions to decide to model some risks in less detail or not at all. Another important reason is the availability and reliability of data. Finally, the feasibility of improvements in risk measurement methods differs across risk types. To get a deeper understanding of the reliability of the parameters, institutions use sensitivity analyses and determine confidence intervals.

To give a general, and thus at points crude, impression of the overall reliability of models for the various risk types, participating institutions have ranked their models on both the banking and the insurance side on a relative scale. The scores are shown in Figure 11 where the relative size of the spheres and the number within the sphere reflect how frequent scores were given. Thus, for instance, for credit risk on the banking side, three institutions ranked credit risk models second (to market risk) and one institution ranked it third.

Figure 11 shows that, especially on the banking side, market risk models are thought to be the most reliable. For credit risk, the

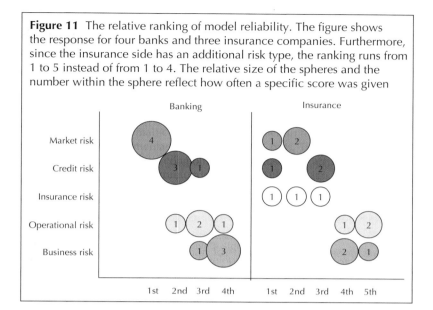

Figure 11 The relative ranking of model reliability. The figure shows the response for four banks and three insurance companies. Furthermore, since the insurance side has an additional risk type, the ranking runs from 1 to 5 instead of from 1 to 4. The relative size of the spheres and the number within the sphere reflect how often a specific score was given

views of the institutions diverge, especially on the insurance side. It is important to note, however, that the importance of credit risk for insurers is limited. For insurance risk, results differ considerably. Some institutions feel that the model for this risk type is the most reliable while others rank it lower, even down to third place. Operational risk models are on average considered reasonably dependable on the banking side but are generally thought to be the least reliable on the insurance side. Finally, business risk is the risk type with the least reliable models on the banking side while on the insurance side these models are deemed to be just as reliable as the models used in operational risk. Interestingly, consensus seems to be closer on the baking side than on the insurance side. On the banking side, the hierarchy revealed runs from market risk to credit risk, operational and finally business risk. Opinions are much more diverse on the insurance side.

APPROACHES PER RISK TYPE
Market or ALM risk
Management action. For market risk and ALM risk, management action is explicitly modelled by all institutions. This means that

liquidity (time-to-close) and binding limit structures, for instance, are incorporated. Moreover, reductions of limits are sometimes included in the analysis.

Assumptions. For market risk, all institutions make the assumptions necessary to apply a one-day VAR calculation in their bank activities. In insurance VARs are generally calculated for a one-year horizon directly. In scaling up to the one-year number, the VAR realisations are assumed to be independent over time. In addition, some Monte Carlo simulations are employed, taking into account management intervention. As noted in the "Time horizon and confidence level" section, models for this risk type in insurance are generally calculated for a one-year horizon directly.

Information on performance and risk drivers. For market risk, many years of history of the underlying risk drivers (interest rates, exchange rates, etc) are available (15 years and up) but shorter periods are used to calculate the VAR. For backtesting, longer periods are used than for the VAR calculation but generally less than the full sample.

Use of external data. Market prices are taken from commercial providers such as Bloomberg, DataStream and Reuters.

Inclusion of risk self-assessment. None of the institutions use risk self-assessment in a systematic way in measuring market or ALM risk.

Consistency. The models are consistent across the banking and the insurance side.

Validation. There are several possible methods to test the validity of the models used, for example backtesting, scenario analysis or benchmarking. Most institutions use all three methods in assessing the solidity of market risk and ALM models. For market risk models in particular, backtesting is widely used. Some institutions build a scenario-based module to stress the event risk exposure that an institution has in the trading books on the banking side. In such an approach, aggregation methods are used to come to a consolidated Event VAR exposure, different from the consolidated VAR exposure. The approach is based on a number of basic scenarios and several methods of accumulating these scenarios, such that they cover a wide range of trading positions the institution takes or could take. The outcomes of these different computations are then compared. Scenarios and parameters are set and reviewed regularly. To gauge the reliability of the parameters, sensitivity analyses are performed. In addition, confidence intervals are determined. On the insurance side, extreme interest rate scenarios are used on the ALM positions.

Credit risk

Management action. Management action is not explicitly modelled. Some institutions note that ideally rating triggers should be modelled as well.

Assumptions. In modelling UL in credit risk, institutions make assumptions about the parameters. PD is in most cases not calculated directly, but associated with a credit rating that has been assigned to a counterparty; in some cases PDs are estimated directly through models such as Moody's KMV. In modelling, PDs for some institutions model valuation and credit migration. A common practice is that once an obligor is in default, obligors will, upon completion of a possible restructuring, only return as new obligors. Finally, EAD is assumed to be non-stochastic and hence does not exhibit any dynamics around a default. In addition to the assumptions about the parameters, institutions make assumptions about the shape of the distribution – especially the tail – reflecting correlations, for instance. Only some institutions' models include covenants and only on a limited scale. In the case that data is missing either benchmark external data is used or, for instance, PD, LGD and EAD are determined by expert judgement.

Information on performance and risk drivers. Institutions have between two to seven years of credit history available on the banking side. On the insurance side the range is, in most cases, somewhat lower.

Use of external data. Moody's KMV is the most frequently mentioned external data provider. In addition, independent rating agencies such as Moody's and Standard & Poor's (S&P) supply information as well.

Inclusion of risk self-assessment. Some institutions use expert judgements to determine the value of particular parameter values if data is missing.

Consistency. In principle, all institutions have a consistent approach within the banking and the insurance side. However, in some cases, historical reasons, implementation difficulties, materiality or the availability of the required data prevents a consistent implementation across both sectors. In general, it is the case that the credit risk models that are developed on the banking side are then implemented on the insurance side.

Validation. For credit risk, all institutions use backtesting and benchmarking to validate the models used. Half of the institutions employ scenario analyses as well. The advantage of scenario analysis over stress testing is that one-off surprises in terms of a realised state-of-the-world (eg, two consecutive quarters of negative growth, etc) are easier to explain than rather arbitrary shocks to risk drivers. The focus of the backtesting exercise is, for some institutions, on establishing the accuracy of the EL component. Furthermore, the accuracy of PD, LGD and EAD are also assessed in some cases.

Insurance risk (both life and P&C)
The approaches implemented for life insurance, on the one hand, and P&C or non-life insurance risk on the other, have very similar characteristics and will thus be discussed in a single section.

Management action. Management action is not explicitly modelled.

Assumptions. Some institutions straightforwardly apply the assumptions made by regulators in their risk-based solvency supervision. Other institutions make particular assumptions about how, for instance, to distinguish between trend and level uncertainty.

Information on performance and risk drivers. Institutions have at least 10 years of loss data but some institutions have, for individual business units, up to 50 years of data. For P&C or non-life insurance risk the available data series are somewhat shorter on the whole. The impact of the shorter series for P&C and non-life is relatively limited, given that trend uncertainty is generally less of an issue (compared with life risk).

Use of external data. Presently, relatively little external data is used in insurance risk. An exception is the use of external mortality tables and trends in these tables. These are generally applied to the institution's own cohort structure. Other external sources may for instance be demographic data from government agencies.

Inclusion of risk self-assessment. None of the institutions use self-assessment in insurance risks.

Consistency. In general, the approaches are consistent although some institutions do not set all relevant parameters centrally. Local (risk) management is thus capable to set parameters to capture the nature and specific features of the business within each unit.

Validation. Only some institutions use backtesting and benchmarking in assessing the accuracy of the risk models in life insurance. Most institutions do not use any of the discussed validation tools. For those institutions that do, it is a regular activity of the insurance risk management function. Thus business units are required to test the adequacy of their reserves under moderately adverse scenarios at least annually. For business units where adequacy is viewed as a potential issue, reserve adequacy testing is computed on a higher frequency. Some institutions use specific models for non-life fire line of business to assess catastrophe risk as a result of storms, fires or earthquakes. The outcomes are used to update external catastrophe re-insurance programs.

Operational risk

Management action. Management action is not explicitly modelled.

Assumptions. An important assumption in using historical data is that it provides a sufficiently accurate picture of future risks. Besides this point, no particular issues were raised.

Information on performance and risk drivers. Most institutions have operational loss data for about four years. Some institutions, however, have up to 25 years of data available. The frequency of measurement and the definitions of events are, however, not entirely stable over time. On the insurance side, some institutions use benchmarks instead of internally generated data.

Use of external data. External data is widely used in operational risk measurement to add to internal data. Market leaders in providing external data are ORX and OpVantage. The latter provides a database (composed of the preceding Netrisk and PriceWaterhouse loss database) that contains publicised operational incidents world-wide of at least US$1 million.

Inclusion of risk self-assessment. Particularly in the area of operational risk, all institutions use self-assessment in some form or other. Sometimes these self-assessments are more formalised and involve a group of experts.

Consistency. The models are consistent across the banking and the insurance side.

Validation. Again, the approaches taken differ across institutions because this is an area that is in development. Backtesting is used by half of the institutions, although in some cases only for average losses, not economic capital. One other institution is planning to use this tool in the future. Scenario analysis is used by one institution while another institution just started. Finally, benchmarking is used by the majority of institutions.

Business or strategic risk

Management action. Management action is not taken into account. This is not surprising given that the time horizon of economic capital modelling is relatively short compared to the time that management action would need to have any effect on the business or strategic risk of an institution.

Assumptions. Institutions use widely differing assumptions, reflecting the various approaches chosen.

Information on performance and risk drivers. Institutions have between 4 and 11 years of data, although the latter number is applicable for an aggregated series.

Use of external data. Some institutions use external benchmarks (ie, industry figures).

Inclusion of risk self-assessment. Not all, but most institutions use self-assessments in some way. Some institutions ask business units to, for instance, choose the revenue drivers and sensitivities.

Consistency. Similar to the other risk types, institution aim to achieve complete consistency across both sectors. Some institutions, however, note that although the approaches are consistent within the sector, it is currently not feasible to implement a single methodology. This implies that, at the group level, there is in some cases a data need that cannot be made available for the whole group.

Validation. Similar to operational risk, approaches differ widely: one institution uses backtesting, scenario analyses and benchmarking while another uses none of these. Other institutions use just backtesting or (have just started using) benchmarking.

FUTURE EXTENSIONS

As technology and insights develop in the future, institutions see further, incremental development of the present modelling techniques. These developments will lead institutions to refine the information requirements risk management. Bringing this information together in a centralised data warehouses will, for the example of credit exposures, enable methodologies to consistently incorporate additional risk drivers (sector and county), thus producing better measures of concentration risk and systematic risk.

Some institutions are developing models to capture funding liquidity risk. There is, however, no consensus on what the role of such a model would be in an economic capital environment. Although well capitalised, banks will have easier access to additional funds in case of liquidity shortage; capital is not seen as the primary defence against such a shortage.

CONCLUDING REMARKS

The survey has uncovered a wealth of information about the state-of-play of the implementation of economic capital models at large Dutch financial conglomerates. A discussion of this material has uncovered a number of important commonalities. All participating institutions have a model in place that produces an economic capital amount, estimated to be sufficient to cover ULs at some predefined confidence level. The economic capital models are used for, for instance, capital allocation, performance measurement and external reporting. The relative importance of each of these purposes differs by institution, however.

Another commonality is that institutions have conceptually consistent models for each risk type across sectors. Practical considerations might lead to slightly different implementation in parts of the conglomerate, however. An example is the implementation of market risk VAR models. On the banking side these models have a relatively long history but have a short time-horizon, due to their risk management roots and the relatively short holding period of trading positions. To come to an estimate of the annual VAR, the short-term VAR numbers are scaled up, using some formula. On the insurance side, legacy models are less of an issue and thus the models for market risk tend to be capable of computing annual VAR numbers directly.

To gauge the reliability of models, participating institutions have ranked the models used for each of the five risk types discerned. This ranking revealed that there is more or less a consensus among participating institutions about the relative reliability of the models for each risk type on the banking side; market risk is placed first, followed by credit, operational and business risk. In contrast, the institutions have more divergent views on the insurance side. Overall, market, credit and insurance risk are deemed to be more reliable than operational and business risk. Within the former three risk types, however, the views of the three participating institutions that are active in the insurance sector are slightly at odds; all three risk types are chosen as the most reliable model at least once.

For many of the risk types modelling is developing at a steady pace. In implementing the models, institutions have chosen to first concentrate on models on the banking side. This is mainly driven by the priorities following from the timelines associated with the implementation of the Basel Capital Adequacy Framework (Basel II). To qualify for the more advanced approaches under Basel, banks have to realise a timely implementation of credit and operational risk models. On the insurance side, Solvency II will also introduce a more risk-based framework and although the Solvency II project is still in a formative phase, the general framework is already clear. Solvency II is thus likely to be a similar stimulus to modelling efforts on the insurance side.

Authors of this chapter:
Iman van Lelyveld, DNB; Moncef Boughanmi, Rabobank; Henk van Broekhoven, ING Group; Hugo Everts, ING Group; Maarten Gelderman, DNB; Olav Jones, Fortis; Pieter Klaassen, ABN AMRO; Hartwig Liersch, ING Group; Raymond Monnik, Rabobank; André Pouw, Fortis; Gaston Siegelaer, DNB and Henrico Wanders Unive Verzekeringen.

1   See the Societies of Acturaries website: rmtf.soa.org/rmtf_ecca.html
2   The feasibility of obtaining sufficient data is always an issue. Quoting from Bernstein (1996, p 202): The information.

The information you have is not the information you want.
The information you want is not the information you need.
The information you need is not the information you can obtain.
The information you can obtain costs more than you want to pay.

6

A Supervisory View on Economic Capital Models

Iman van Lelyveld

The chapters so far have been primarily concerned with the technical issues of how to measure and aggregate risks, and subsequently how to determine capital need(s), followed by a survey of the state-of-play of economic capital modelling at Dutch financial conglomerates. Now we will discuss an application of economic capital models that has – as yet – to gain widespread acceptance, namely regulatory use. Developments in industry and in the supervisory arena have made the discussion about the use of economic capital models for regulatory use timely and useful, as economic capital models could deliver important information for all stakeholders.

A prerequisite for regulatory use of economic capital models would seem to be that institutions themselves put sufficient faith in these internal models. Are these models, or seen more broadly, is risk management adequately embedded in the organisation? This implies that the ultimate responsibility for the model used, lies with the institution. Moreover, that senior management understands and approves the overall approach chosen (ie, determines the risk preference). It also implies a clear and documented delineation of responsibilities. A true acid test is whether the institution incorporates model outcomes in other processes such as pricing or performance related pay.

Supervisors will, in addition to the appropriate embedding within the institution, have to be attentive to a number of issues. The most important of these are the effects of recognising economic capital model use on competitive equality, the behaviour of the models in times of stress, and, finally, the home-host aspect of model and model outcome recognition. These and other issues will be discussed in more detail in the present chapter.

Notwithstanding the above mentioned and other concerns, introducing economic capital models in the supervisory framework does provide a positive stimulant to improving risk awareness, measurement and management. By itself this development will not immediately solve all the imperfections in risk management we see today but given time it will certainly improve risk management.

INTRODUCTION

The economic capital models we have studied in the previous chapters promise to deliver different things to different stakeholders:

❑ For the institutions implementing the models, they promise to deliver a view on the risk profile and the associated capital needed. Given that capital need, the model is then used to allocate capital across business units.
❑ For supervisors, these models could help improve understanding of the true capital needed rather than exclusively focusing on more mechanically determined regulatory minimum capital requirements.
❑ For capital market participants, economic capital numbers would give a more accurate picture of the true risk profile of an institution as well.
❑ For policyholders and deposit holders, economic capital numbers would give them an indication whether the institution is able to deliver the services now and in the future that were agreed upon.

Given the insights gained in the drafting of the papers to date, it is now time to turn our attention to one use economic capital models generally have not, as yet, been put to: supervisory use. The interest to use internal models is increasing among regulators and supervisors. An early contribution in this respect is a Supervisory and Regulation Letter published by the Federal Reserve Board of Governors (Board of Governors of the Federal Reserve System (1999)). In banking, institutions may use (upon qualifying) some of the same parameters in computing regulatory minimum capital requirements as in internal capital determination under the first pillar in the new Basel Capital Adequacy Framework (BCBS 2005). Moreover, in the second pillar of the Basel Framework economic capital models are likely to form the core of the compulsory Internal Capital Adequacy Assessment Process (ICAAP). Similarly, on the insurance side, the Solvency II regulatory framework also contains three pillars and has room for internal models (even in the first pillar). A conceptual difference between Solvency II and Basel II that we will discuss more thoroughly later on is that in the former approach all risks are expected to be covered in the first pillar, while in the Basel II approach some of the risks are specifically placed in the second pillar.

Supervisors might use economic capital models to come to a view on the risk profile and associated capital, or more precisely, determine regulatory capital.[1] This would herald a shift from the traditional accounting-based approach to capital to an economic-value-based approach. In the former approach, the buffer capital is defined in accounting terms, generally against historical prices, while in the latter approach buffer capital is the difference in economic value between assets and liabilities against market or, alternatively, fair values. During the transition from accounting to value-based approaches tensions will emerge and these should be dealt with if and when they arise.

Several options are open to supervisors in accepting models and model outcomes. On one end of the spectrum, supervisors could take the model outcomes at face value and set regulatory capital requirements equal or proportional to economic capital. Another approach is that supervisors would critically assess the model and would only allow certain models or constrain parameter values to be within certain ranges. Yet another approach to using these models is that supervisors would incorporate economic capital outcomes as one of many pieces of information in coming to a proper assessment of the risk profile of an institution. This chapter will conclude that neither polar case is applicable but that economic capital models are well worth incorporating in the supervisory assessment process.

Notwithstanding the clear advantages of supervisory use of economic capital models there are a number of issues that make unconditional incorporation of model outcomes less straightforward. The most important of these considerations are the behaviour of the models in times of stress, the possibly less than complete coverage of the models, concerns about the organisational embedding of the risk management process, and, finally, the home-host aspect of model and model outcome recognition. These and other arguments will be discussed in subsequent sections.

To give adequate attention to all these issues, the chapter has the following structure. First, the developments within the regulatory arena are sketched as a background. It will be argued that recent changes have been conducive to the discussion of economic capital for regulatory purposes. Then we will pay attention to the general (organisational) framework of economic capital models. The way the models are embedded within organisations is important to supervisors because this supplies additional checks on and correct incentives in the model, if implemented appropriately. This is followed by setting out the broader objectives that supervisors are pursuing followed by a discussion of a number of issues that are of particular concern to supervisors. Finally, we conclude.

REGULATORY DEVELOPMENTS

So far, the chapters have focused on the developments within the industry that might eventually lead to an industry standard. In the mean time, a number of important developments have taken place in the regulatory arena as well. Our discussion is focused on the European developments as for most financial conglomerates in the Netherlands that is where most activities are located. Similarly to most countries elsewhere, the legal basis for the supervision of banks and insurers in European countries remains strictly sectoral. However, this sector-based regulatory environment is changing rapidly. A first example is the implementation of the Financial Conglomerates Directive in the EU member states. The Financial Conglomerates Directive allows for further information exchange among supervisors and emphasises the view on capital from the holding company's perspective. A second example is the convergence of approaches in both Capital Requirements Directive (CRD), the EU law implementing the Basel Capital Adequacy Framework) and the Solvency II process. In both of these approaches for the banking and the insurance sectors, the general framework consists of three similar pillars. Moreover, both Solvency II and the CRD are likely to contain elements that would ease acceptance of economic capital. For instance, parameters used in economic capital models have found their way into the advanced approaches for credit risk in the CRD. Finally, a third example is the trend in many countries to merge sectoral supervisory agencies and where sectoral supervisors have merged, supervisory practices are likely to converge across sectors. Taken together these developments make the acceptance of economic capital models (somewhat) more likely and we will now discuss each of these three developments – the conglomerates directive, the CRD and Solvency II, and supervisory institutional structure – in more detail.

The Financial Conglomerates Directive

One step in overcoming the tremendous difficulties of coming to a consistent regulatory framework, at least within Europe, was the implementation of the Financial Conglomerates Directive. This Directive was enacted in the European Economic Area (EEA) member states in autumn 2004 for application to financial years beginning on 1st January 2005. The Directive introduced supplementary supervision of financial conglomerates on a group-wide basis in order to address some of the concerns voiced. It operates in addition to both the prudential supervision of EEA regulated entities on a stand-alone basis and consolidated supervision on a sectoral basis.

The directive applies to firms that qualify according to the following two steps: a group only qualifies as a financial conglomerate if: (a) more than 50% of group activities are financial, and (b) the shares of the banking sector (including security activities) and the insurance sector in the total of the financial activities are each within 10–90%. In addition, if the minority share has a balance sheet larger than €6 billion, the group also qualifies as a financial conglomerate. If the group is headed by an unregulated entity, it is called a mixed financial holding. A procedure is given for identifying the co-ordinator, which is generally the regulator of the parent undertaking heading a financial conglomerate.[2]

The co-ordinator has a number of methods at his disposal, the main options being:

❏ supplementary supervision of the conglomerate's capital adequacy, including requirements at the holding level;
❏ requiring periodic reporting of significant risk concentrations at the holding level;

❑ requiring periodic reporting of significant intra-group transactions (those above 5% of the financial conglomerate's capital requirement are presumed significant).

In addition, the requirement for management to be of sufficiently good repute and experience is extended to the management of a financial holding company with at least one regulated EEA subsidiary.

One of the important aspects of the Financial Conglomerates Directive is that it will make exchange of information among parties with a legitimate interest easier. Once stakeholders have gained some experience in this process, the advantages of conducting this dialogue within a single consistent framework, ie, economic capital, might be more easily recognised.

Regarding possible capital allocation and structure effects, caused by the introduction of the financial conglomerates directive, we will discuss briefly the relevant articles from the directive. First, apart from the sectoral rules, the directive introduces supplementary supervision of the capital adequacy of the regulated entities in a financial conglomerate. The supervisor shall require regulated entities in a financial conglomerate to ensure that own funds are available at the level of the financial conglomerate that are always at least equal to the capital adequacy requirements. At the level of the financial conglomerate, adequate capital adequacy policies shall be in place.[3]

Relevant technical principles[4] indicate the following additional solvency requirements:

❑ where sectoral rules provide for limits on the eligibility of certain own funds instruments, which would qualify as cross-sector capital, these limits would apply *mutatis mutandis* when calculating own funds at the level of the financial conglomerate;
❑ when calculating own funds at the level of the financial conglomerate, competent authorities shall also take into account the effectiveness of the transferability and availability of the own funds across different legal entities in the group, given the objectives of the capital adequacy rules.

Capital Requirements Directive and Solvency II
The Capital Requirements Directive is the EU legislation that will put the legally non-binding Basel agreement into European law. The Directive will, in turn, be put into national law as of 2007. For

the most part, the Directive is substantively equal to the Basel Capital Adequacy Framework. Solvency II is the European Commission's project to achieve harmonisation of risk-based capital requirements within the EU. The details of Solvency II are presently being filled in. For a more detailed treatment of the Solvency II structure, we refer to the Box on Solvency II below.

An important similarity between Solvency II and Basel II is that a three-pillar structure seems to have been chosen in both frameworks; a first pillar with minimum requirements, a second pillar describing the supervisory review process and, finally, a third "disclosure" pillar for promoting market discipline.

Given this framework, the place of internal models is, however, somewhat different within the insurance compared with the banking sector's regulatory framework. Basel II has explicit minimum capital requirements for market, credit, and operational risk. Although the models used to determine regulatory minimum capital requirements do use some of the same inputs, they are not true internal models as supervisors partly determine their workings. In addition, there is the second pillar where, on the one hand, institutions are required to hold sufficient capital for all risks and, on the other hand, supervisors will have to assess the adequacy of this capital adequacy process and its outcome in their Supervisory Review. The Basel second pillar clearly recognises that some risks are not, or are not adequately, captured under the first pillar but should be incorporated in the internal model used in the second pillar. In contrast, in Solvency II the use of an internal model is already envisaged in the first pillar and is thus used to determine the minimum capital requirements. The second pillar is then only reserved for the Supervisory Review, producing a supervisor's view on an institution's risk management, including the adequacy of capital.

The set-up of the supervisory review also influences the appropriate supervisory response to more risk-based capital adequacy approaches. Traditionally supervisors only set an absolute minimum capital requirement. In the supervisory review, as envisaged, supervisors could determine an additional capital requirement either because of additional institution-specific risk or because of systemic risk concerns. Dealing with the separate requirements following from the first and the second pillar merits further development. An important development in this respect is the introduction in Solvency II of the concepts of Minimum Capital Requirement (MCR) and Solvency Capital Requirement (SCR). The former is the absolute minimum; an institution with capital below this threshold forfeits its license. The latter is the target solvency level that an institution should generally be able to maintain.

SOLVENCY II: THE CURRENT STATE-OF-PLAY

Although the development of the Solvency II project is still in full swing, an outline is becoming clear. In this box we will first provide some historical background of (European) insurance supervision and then sketch the current state of play.

What is the problem?

The core activity in insurance is the transfer of risks from clients to the insurance company. By pooling these risks, the insurer can charge a premium based on the "average" insured customer. Insurance has an inverse product cycle: the premium is generally received (much) earlier than the insured risks materialise. An insurance company typically invest the premiums received in order to be able to pay out later. Therefore, there are two main risks in insurance. On the one hand, there is uncertainty around the timing and size of future payments (insurance risk) and, on the other hand, uncertainty around the value of the invested assets and the value of the – insurance – liabilities over time (mismatch risk). Keeping these risks in check is a core activity in insurance and recently many firms have invested heavily in risk models, preferably for the entire institution. Especially in the life insurance business, it is important to adjust the investment policy to the expected pay outs stemming from the often long termed contracts. These adjustments imply an active ALM policy.

In order to be able to make good on their insurance liabilities, insurers maintain both technical provisions – more precisely; assets to cover technical provisions – and capital. The technical provisions are essentially a reflection of the expected future outgoing cash flows implied by current contracts. In addition, insurers hold capital to cover unexpected expenses. The financial position of an insurer, and therefore the degree to which an insurer will be able to make good on (future) promises, is thus reflected by the sum of total technical provisions and capital. These two components, technical provisions and capital, are central to the prudential supervision of insurers.

The current solvency requirements for European insurers date from the seventies. In those days, insurers sold relatively simple products and, subsequently, invested the proceeds in a number of basic investment instruments. The regulatory requirements reflect this rather simple business model and are therefore also relatively easy to implement.

Over time, a number of additions and changes have been implemented, such as the introduction of supplementary group supervision. An important motivation for these changes was to stimulate the single European market.

A marked change is that insurers are now selling increasingly complex products and are investing in a much wider range of financial instruments, supported by the development of risk management systems. The current, rather simple regulatory requirements have not yet incorporated these market developments and do not adequately capture the risk profile of the typical insurer. The three main shortcomings are that:

1. The financial regulatory requirements do not adequately capture the risk profile of an insurer. Only the size of the operation is relevant in determining the capital requirement. As premium income or pay outs (P&C insurance) or technical provisions (life insurance) rise, the capital requirement also rises. Investment risks are only reflected in the discount rate used in the determination of the technical provisions. As such, this discount rate can be seen as a proxy for the expected return. This implies that an insurer with a risky investment strategy does not have to maintain a higher regulatory capital buffer. Alternatively, an insurer which actively and successfully manages its risks does not see this reflected in a lower capital requirement. Recent developments in bond and equity markets have shown the dangers inherent in the current approach.
2. There is a lack of transparency about how technical provisions are determined. Both the methodology used in determining the provisions and the degree of certainty with which the buffers should be able to withstand shocks differ. This makes comparisons between firms very difficult.
3. The freedom to choose a valuation methodology. The balance sheet does not give an adequate view of the institution's risk profile as market or fair values are not yet widely used.

Naturally, supervisors, the actuarial profession and the sector have fine-tuned the existing regulatory framework. These "patches" have created a functioning system that has been helpful in keeping the number of accidents to a minimum. It implies that practical solutions have been found to address issues that are not clear in the regulations. However, the sense that a more fundamental overhaul of the system is needed, has been growing. The Solvency II project is intended to take care of this.

The outline of Solvency II
Presently, the outline of Solvency is emerging. Similar to Basel II it will have a three-pillar structure. The first pillar contains the capital requirements, based on quantifiable risk categories. The second pillar is the *supervisory review*. In this *review* the supervisor assesses the

firm's organisational structure, whether the complete risk profile has been adequately captured, and whether controls are adequately implemented throughout the firm. The third pillar, finally, focuses on market discipline through public disclosure by the insurer of relevant information to the public.

Although the three pillar structure seems to be conceptually similar to the structure chosen for the Basel Framework, there are a number of practical differences. One difference is that in Solvency II project it is the explicit intention to have all measurable risks in the first pillar, and hence require capital for them. In the Basel framework, only market-, credit-, and operational risk are included in the first pillar. It is likely that, at the very least, insurance risk and the most important investment risks (interest rate risk, credit risk, etc.) will be included in the Solvency II first pillar. Possibly, liquidity risk will be tackled in the second pillar. Compared to banks this risk is generally less of an issue for insurers.

Another difference between Solvency II and Basel II is that Solvency II has two capital requirements. A minimum capital requirement (*Minimum Capital Requirement* or *MCR*) and a more risk sensitive capital requirement (*Solvency Capital Requirement* or *SCR*). The MCR is intended to be a simple and robust measure. Furthermore, it should be an absolute minimum and breaking this barrier should trigger severe supervisory action, possibly leading to closure. The role of the MCR, and the risks to be included in this measure, are however not clear presently. The SCR is the capital level with which the insurer is able to withstand shocks with a high degree of certainty (99.5%) over a time horizon of one year. The liabilities are naturally projected over the full contractual length. In the case of a life insurance product this could be a several decades. Furthermore, a holistic approach is chosen: what are the consequences for the surplus (assets – liabilities) of an insurance firm? If the investments are tightly matched, then shocks to risk drivers will not significantly affect the surplus value. In that case the required capital will be low. The insurer should in any case comply with the SCR. If the actual funds drop below the SCR, then the insurer will face increased supervisory scrutiny. The details of this procedure still have to be decided, however.

Solvency II intends to have a close match between the risk profile of the institution and regulatory capital requirements. This, in turn, should stimulate professional risk management. Therefore, Solvency II allows the use of an internal model to calculate the SCR. A requirement is that the insurer has the expertise, the data and the infrastructure necessary to develop, implement and use these models. Solvency II will in principle allow models for all risk in the first pillar. Moreover, partial models will also be allowed. Such partial models would combine standard, supervisory models for some risks with truly internal models for other risks. One could think of for instance a casualty insurer, mainly active in catastrophe insurance, which would have an advanced and refined model for insurance risk. For investment risk, however, it would use a simple model. Solvency II will also allow for models that determine SCR on a group level. The capital requirements based on the internal model can be lower than those following from the standard method. Both the internal model and the standard method comprise essentially the same risks but the more detailed analysis (and improved risk management) can lead to lower capital charges.

Under Solvency II, the assessment of the capital requirements is based on the information in the balance sheet at market valuation. For insurance liabilities, however, a sufficiently liquid market does not exist. Therefore these liabilities will have to valued with alternative methods. These alternative methods should be in line with 'fair value' principles. Basically, the approach is to take the expected value of all future cash flows, discount these using the risk free rate, resulting in a best estimate. Then a risk margin is added to incorporate the uncertainty of the future cash flows.

Figure 12 The relationship between the various requirements

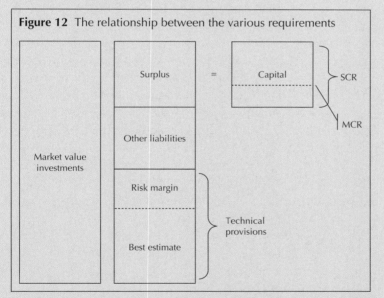

The computation and calibration of the provisions, the MCR and the SCR should be considered together. Although the risk margin is part of the market-consistent value of technical provisions, it does not necessarily come into play in determining the MCR and/or SCR. It is currently being debated what risks should be reflected in which financial requirement. A fundamental issue is whether the MCR should be sensitive to mismatch risk (the risk that investments are not properly aligned to (insurance) liabilities.

Institutional structure of supervision

The structure of financial sector supervision has seen some changes recently, both on the national as well as on the international level. Internationally, at least in Europe, the further structure as given by the Lamfalussy structure has recently been introduced and details are currently being filled in. This structure was proposed by the *Committee of Wise Men on the Regulation of European Securities Markets*, chaired by Baron Lamfalussy. The Committee was set up in July 2000 by the Economic and Finance Ministers of the EU (ECOFIN) with a mandate to assess the current conditions for the implementation of securities' markets regulation in the EU and to propose improvements in order to ensure greater convergence and co-operation in day-to-day implementation of EU-wide regulation. A full description of these changes is unfeasible given the limitations of this chapter but broadly speaking the proposals are based on a new, four-level regulatory approach, aiming to establish faster and more flexible decision-making procedures for securities market legislation and to ensure the uniform application of Community Law. The European Parliament endorsed the four-level approach, which was extended to the other financial sectors, the banking sector included (see Commission 2005). The CEBS and the Committee of European Insurance and Occupational Pensions Supervisors (CEIOPS) are the main committees for EU supervisors aiming at further EU-wide convergence of supervisory practices in the banking and insurance sectors, respectively. The third level three committee, the Committee of European Securities Supervisors (CESR), is responsible for regulating securities (trading) and undertakings for collective investment in transferable securities (UCITS). The Lamfalussy approach does not change the existing institutional setting but clarifies the roles and responsibilities of the various players leading to better advice to the legislative authorities.

On the national level, a number of countries have recently reorganised the institutional structure of supervision.[5] A general trend that can be discerned is that in many countries cross-sectoral regulatory agencies are being created. Although variations exist, these agencies tend to take two forms: full integration of all supervisory authorities, or concentration by supervisory function. The first model, implemented in the United Kingdom, for instance, amounts to merging all supervisory agencies together in one agency and leaving the central bank in charge of monetary policy, including the function of lender-of-last-resort. A variation is the solution chosen in Ireland where all supervisory functions have been merged within the central bank. The functional model, on the other hand, distinguishes between market conduct and prudential supervision. Prudential supervision is entrusted to one agency, possibly within the central bank, and the responsibility for market-conduct supervision is given to a separate organisation. The latter model has recently been implemented in the Netherlands (Prast and Van Lelyveld 2005).

For our present analysis, the most important aspect of the reorganisation is the combination of (line-) supervision within a single supervisory agency. Similarly to financial conglomerates, this forces supervisors in both sectors to align supervisory approaches. A first step here is to come to a single method of risk analysis. This method comprises a risk typology akin to the classification in the first chapter. Second, the risk analysis method at DNB produces a risk profile for each institution. In this sense, it can be seen as a qualitative version of the economic capital models that we have been discussing so far. Once a unified risk analysis method has been implemented, it is easier to make supervisory approaches converge in both sectors. Nevertheless, even in institutions where the responsibilities for banking and insurance have been combined for quite some time, the supervisory approach does not have to be identical across sectors. This implies that the regulatory treatment of similar risks might differ over sectors.

PRINCIPLES FOR ECONOMIC CAPITAL MODELS
Introduction
The discussion in the chapters so far has mainly dealt with how the appropriate level of economic capital can be determined. The broader question as to what would constitute good first principles that would guarantee that the model is properly embedded has not yet been dealt with explicitly. As noted before, the economic capital model discussion shows great similarity to the discussion presently taking place within CEBS about the ICAAP. CEBS has recently released a number of High Level Principles that set out principles to

which institutions should adhere in the development and maintenance of their ICAAP (see CEBS 2004). Paraphrasing these principles in the context of economic capital models leads to the following:

1. the economic capital model is the institution's responsibility;
2. the economic capital model should be proportionate to the nature, size, risk profile and complexity of the institution;
3. the economic capital model should capture all of the material risks;
4. the economic capital model should be included in a formal and documented procedure, including the role of the management body;
5. the economic capital model should as far as possible form an integral part of the management process and decision-making culture of the institution and it should be properly embedded in the organisation;
6. the economic capital model should be reviewed regularly, at least annually, by an independent party;
7. the economic capital model should be comprehensive and representative;
8. the economic capital model should as far as possible be forward-looking;
9. the economic capital model should produce a reasonable outcome.

Not all of these principles are equally relevant to our present discussion. Principle 2, for instance, is aimed at the many smaller financial institutions that would also be expected to have an ICAAP in place. However, these smaller institutions generally have a simple risk profile and this would therefore lead supervisors to expect a less complicated model, in combination with measures to ensure that no undue risks are taken in areas that have been modelled in a less sophisticated way. Other principles are quite relevant, however, and we will therefore discuss each of them in the next section.

High level principles: further detail
1. *The economic capital model is the institution's responsibility.* Even if an economic capital model is used in setting regulatory capital,

ownership should still be with the institution. The economic capital model should be a means of supporting the dialogue between the supervisory authority and the institution. Moreover, a continuous dialogue between the institution's senior management and the risk-management department is of great importance in this context. The dialogue touches the trade-off between "measuring" and "controlling". An adequate internal model that has been properly deployed by a risk-management department reveals the risks that the institution is running. It is then the responsibility of senior management, based on the work of the risk management department, to shape the control of those risks by means of specific policy decisions.

2. *The economic capital model should be proportionate to the nature, size, risk profile and complexity of the institution.* Establishing whether the economic capital model in fact complies with this principle, should be established on a case-by-case basis. In this review, aspects such as the institution's legal form or its significance to financial stability may also play a role. As noted, however, this principle is more relevant in the general EU CRD discussion, which is also applicable to a large number of small institutions.

3. *The economic capital model should capture all of the material risks.* The range of risks discerned has been discussed in the first chapter. Naturally, the relative weights will differ for each individual institution. In addition to the risk types, the institution's risk preference should be incorporated in the assessment of the risks.

Furthermore, it is not just the risks that are easy to model quantitatively that should be incorporated; risks requiring a more qualitative approach should ideally also have to be included. One way would be to use expert judgement, although how to go about this seems to be an unsettled question. In addition, the view that the final economic capital model only includes material risks does not absolve the institution from its obligation to demonstrate that the excluded risks are not material. This should preclude "cherry-picking" by only modelling those areas with relatively little risk.

In determining capital requirements, capital needs in stressed situations should explicitly be incorporated. Sensitivity to those situations, and the associated required capital, can be assessed using stress tests. Senior management or a dedicated committee must be actively involved in drawing up and evaluating the stress tests. If these stress tests show that the institution is susceptible to certain risks, prompt action must follow to properly control the changed risk profile.

4. *The economic capital model should be included in a formal and documented procedure, including the role of the management body.* As an institution's senior management has final responsibility for the economic capital model, senior management must approve its conceptual design (at least the objectives and scope of the model and, generally, the methodology). Further development can be carried out under the responsibility of the executive management. The methodology of assumptions in and procedures surrounding the economic capital model need to be established and approved by the senior management. Management should also be responsible for integrating the economic capital model and its outcomes in the management culture. It is therefore important, as noted in the next principle, that (the outcome of) the economic capital model is promoted within the organisation with sufficient commitment. The final outcome of the economic capital model should be reported periodically and regularly to senior management. The frequency of reporting depends on the assumed speed at which the risk profile changes.

5. *The economic capital model should, as far as possible, form an integral part of the management process and decision-making culture of the institution.* In short, it should be properly embedded in the organisation. Similar to all models, the outcome of an economic capital model depends crucially on the information that is fed into the model. The quality of information, in turn, depends on the effort exerted to assure that this information accurately reflects current exposures and associated risk. The institution thus must have procedures to ensure the quality, promptness and completeness of data input. The integrity of the data process must be evaluated regularly. In addition to the processes in place, the effort expended will depend on the importance of the outcome of the model. If the model is merely a cosmetic exercise with no real consequences, the quality of the data will suffer accordingly. If, on the other hand, the model is used in several different and important decision processes,

forces within the organisation will assure that the quality of the data is adequate.

If, however, the incentives produced by the model are perverse, individual personnel or managers might try to game the system. Such perverse behaviour, however, would generally lead to (opportunity) losses elsewhere in the organisation and management in those parts of the organisation would object. Only if risk is not adequately captured and would thus become "invisible" could such risk shifting occur undetected. It is in the interest of senior management to implement a system that uses adequate measurement and produces the appropriate incentives.

Given the incentives of senior management, the model should be implemented with care and should form an integral part of day-to-day risk management and thus of the process of planning, monitoring and controlling the institution's risk profile. Moreover, it should also lead to a well-defined capital plan stipulating the firm's policy in case capital is no longer in line with it's risk profile.[6] Furthermore, there should be a reporting line to the senior decision-making body on the actual risk profile compared with the risk standard. The systems and processes used in operations must be consistent with the economic capital model. The latter applies particularly to risk-management measures as incorporated in the economic capital model.

In particular, more sophisticated institutions can be expected to have integrated the economic capital model in the operating process. For example, this may be done by using the economic capital model for allocating resources to business units, taking individual investment or disposal decisions or more generally for business decisions (such as expansion plans) and budgets. Less sophisticated or smaller institutions may decide to outsource part of the economic capital modelling. Supervisors will, however, be particularly attentive because of the importance of ownership of the capital adequacy process.

6. *The economic capital model should be reviewed regularly, at least annually, by an independent party.* Such a review can ensure that all material risks are properly identified and measured and, therefore, that the economic capital model gives an accurate view of the institution's risk profile. An institution should, therefore, have an independent risk management function responsible for

the design, implementation and maintenance of its internal model. Staff responsible for this function should be independent of the commercial activities, especially when the validity of the model is determined. They should report directly to the institution's senior management and they should critically review whether the models used are sufficiently comprehensive, accurate and prudent. Furthermore, they should initiate improvements to the model as necessary. Finally, they should also ensure the independent review of all material processes applicable to the model such as data collection, qualitative input, etc.

As became clear in the previous chapter on the state of implementation, institutions have chosen different organisational forms to assure that model validation is insulated from undue (commercial) pressure. One issue that became clear is that the traditional auditor is less well equipped to assess an economic capital model. Thus, if the audit department is assigned a significant role in the validation process then audit departments will have to acquire new skill sets. Alternatively, if responsibility for validation is assigned to a unit within risk management then these risk managers will have to become more or less independent; it might be difficult for risk managers to independently validate models if they were closely involved in developing these models. In the end, both organisational forms produce their own challenges.

The fact that some of the economic capital model outcomes are also published in annual reporting, for instance, implies that institutions will be inclined to put more effort in assuring its solidity. General reporting guidelines and regulations, such as those given in the American Sarbanes-Oxley legislation, for instance, have made institutions more attentive to the quality of what is being reported. In this respect there is a permanent reporting quality drive.

7. *The economic capital model should be comprehensive and representative.* The administrative systems should be reviewed as to whether they provide the necessary information, and are reliable and representative of the institution itself. Attention also has to be given to the availability of general, external information and parameters. "Expert judgement" will have to be relied upon where these are not available.

The economic capital model will have to be updated if the assumptions and/or methodology prove to have changed substantially, for example as a result of a different strategic focus, a revised business plan, a changed environment, etc. If new risks occur, they too should be incorporated immediately in the economic capital model. Keeping the economic capital model up to date is, therefore, an ongoing, iterative process.

It is vitally important that not only all material risks are incorporated, but also that they are measured reliably and consistently throughout the institution. Risks must be identified, quantified and managed transparently, consistently and prudently, partly through the economic capital model. When applying the economic capital model, an institution also has to consider its possible limitations. The institution must be able to assess the risks estimated with the model using the appropriate professional expertise. If necessary, internal specialists should adjust model outcomes on the basis of significant information that is not incorporated in the model. There must be a procedure for authorising and documenting these changes. It is useful to have clear guidance at hand especially for risks that are less easy to quantify.

8. *The economic capital model should, as far as, possible be forward-looking.* Most models are estimated using historical data and are, therefore, dependent on the past. It would be commendable if the economic capital model is as forward looking as possible, on the basis of the historical data and other information on the future risk profile (strategic plans, macro-economic forecasts), so that proper projections can be made "through the cycle", for instance. The remark that an economic capital model can be deployed more widely than just merely for establishing solvency levels fits in this context; examples are stress tests and supporting an integrated vision of the institution's future development.

9. *The economic capital model should produce a reasonable outcome.* The institution should have a proper process for validating the accuracy and consistency of the economic capital model. Regular backtesting is part of this. The economic capital model is validated on first use and if and when changes are made to the model, and preferably again some time after this. This validation exercise includes comparing the estimated risks against

actual results. The internal and external data used should be up to date and representative. Moreover, the institution should document the validation results and use these to enhance the quality of the risk analysis. The institution should critically evaluate the performance of the models and aim for improvement, partly by regularly comparing the results from the model against new internal and external information on the modelled risks.

In the end, the outcome of the economic capital model must be approached with a healthy degree of scepticism. Every model is an abstraction of reality. It is, therefore, important that the outcomes of the economic capital model are approached in a structured way and discussed before they are allowed to influence policy. If the supervisory authority has additional information that puts the outcome of the economic capital model in a different light, this has to be included in the discussion and should lead to changes in the assessment of the buffer capital needed.

SUPERVISORY ISSUES
Objectives
Supervisors can pursue a wide range of objectives and the following list seems to capture a broad consensus:

1. promote safety and soundness of the financial system, including safeguarding the economic interest of deposit holders and policyholders;
2. enhance competitive equality;
3. constitute a comprehensive approach to addressing risks;
4. risk sensitive capital requirements;
5. accommodate industry best practice;
6. reduce the cost of implementation of new approaches and of supervision.

Giving economic capital models a prominent role in determining capital requirements can help attaining a number of these objectives. A well-rounded economic capital model is undoubtedly the most comprehensive model of an institution's risks available and would thus fulfil objective number three. Since the model would be risk sensitive, this would also cover objective four. Moreover, economic capital models are at the forefront of risk management technology (objective five), although for some elements, such as the assessment of diversification, consensus on best practice is yet to emerge. If supervisors increasingly rely on the outcomes of internal models for their assessments on the risk profiles of institutions then institutions will have to report a great deal less (basic) data. In this case, supervisors do not have to compute their own, simple models based on reported base data. This, in turn, would reduce reporting and compliance costs, making objective six easier to achieve. The first objective, promoting the safety and soundness of the financial system, would seem to be easier to achieve if economic capital models increase a supervisor's (and institution's) understanding of risks. Moreover, more risk sensitive capital requirements help to ensure that capital is there where it is most needed.

The only objective where it is not entirely clear whether economic capital models are unequivocally beneficial might be objective number two: increased competitive equality. We will turn to this issue in the next section. Furthermore, we will then in subsequent sections raise a number of other issues specific to the use of economic capital models by or for supervisors. These issues are supplementing the explanation of the CEBS' High Level Principles for ICAAP given in the previous section and are, in no particular order, the appropriate confidence level in evaluating the model, going concern and times of stress, the appropriateness of VAR measures, model convergence and limited data availability, partial use, definition of capital and, last but not least, home-host issues.

Competitive equality

As noted in the previous section, objective number two – increased competitive equality – might not benefit unequivocally upon accepting economic capital models for supervisory use. More specifically, two angles can be discerned: (1) competitive equality among large, internationally active financial institutions, and (2) between large and small institutions. We will discuss both of these angles in turn.

Economic capital models are at first likely to be primarily implemented by large, internationally active financial institutions. Furthermore, if supervisors decide to place relatively more weight on the outcomes of economic capital models then the level playing field across jurisdictions becomes increasingly more important. To warrant the level playing field in this regard and increase model understanding, supervisors with a legitimate interest are likely to discuss economic capital models amongst themselves. Thus, without impinging on the home country control principle, some sort of peer review might be useful in increasing supervisors' understanding of economic capital models.

A second angle is that the significant (fixed) costs of economic capital models might drive smaller institutions out of the market and raise entrance barriers for new entrants. This is particular problem for smaller all-round banks. A mitigating factor for smaller niche players might be that a more narrow focus also greatly reduces the complexity of the economic capital model. As an example, one could think of a credit card bank. For such a bank, the economic capital model could be rather simple; ie, adequate modelling of a single portfolio (credit cards) and a model of operational risk. Another mitigating factor might be the possibility that part of the economic capital modelling might be outsourced. However, supervisors are likely to be very attentive of the exact form chosen and make sure that ownership of the capital adequacy process lies with management and outsourcing does not lead to a loss of control or understanding.

The confidence level to be evaluated

The implicit confidence level underlying regulatory frameworks such as Basel II and Solvency II roughly translates to a target of at least an investment grade rating. However, many institutions aim for a rather higher level of confidence. For instance, these institutions target a AA or AAA rating. An issue in the Supervisory Review is whether supervisors should evaluate an institution's risk profile and associated desired capital level at the minimal investment grade confidence level or at the generally higher internal level of confidence.

The impact of the choice of the confidence level can be significant as an example adapted from Hall (2002) shows. In Figure 13 we present a very simple example showing the effect of changing the confidence level. Both portfolios shown have a similar expected loss but the portfolio represented by the solid line has a considerably

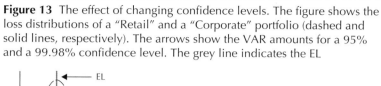

Figure 13 The effect of changing confidence levels. The figure shows the loss distributions of a "Retail" and a "Corporate" portfolio (dashed and solid lines, respectively). The arrows show the VAR amounts for a 95% and a 99.98% confidence level. The grey line indicates the EL

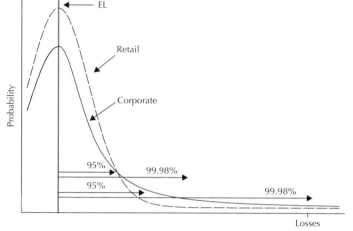

fatter tail. Such a distribution is typical of, for instance, corporate portfolios, while the bottom pane resembles the loss distributions in many retail portfolios. Increasing the confidence level will lead to a significant increase in the VAR amount as indicated by the much larger rightward shift of the 99.98% arrow (in comparison with the 95% arrow). A different confidence level thus implies that whoever evaluates the risk measures will come to a different assessment of the relative risks of portfolios in an institution.

One argument for using the internal target level in the supervisory assessment is that supervisors should be able to understand the risk profile including all risks and that, for example, business risk and funding risk are an integral part of this profile. The targeted rating is an important part of an institutions business model and failing to achieve or, possibly even more damaging, getting a downgrade will severely impact upon an institution's risk profile. A consequence could for instance be that funding for a rating-sensitive business such as swaps dries up. A counterargument, however, is that even though in the second pillar the supervisor should evaluate the whole risk profile, consistency with the first pillar should also be maintained. And since under the first pillar investment grade is sufficient, supervisors should not be overly zealous.

Going concern and times of stress

An issue of particular interest to supervisors is the amount of capital needed in case of stress levels exceeding the levels used to calculate capital adequacy. The question is then to what extent the model can be relied upon in times of crisis. To put it differently, does the model still reflect the actual risk profile in a severely stressed market? It has been argued for instance that in such circumstances correlations between risk drivers, that in normal times exhibit low correlation, would increase significantly, possibly approaching a value of 1. This would in turn mean that any diversification benefits would be lost when they are especially needed.

One way to approach this issue is to devise and implement sensitivity and stress tests. Although such tests are to a degree arbitrary, given the lucky circumstance that institutions only have limited historical information on truly stressful periods, stress tests do provide some insights into the effects of increasing correlations between risks, for instance.

Another reaction to this issue is the argument that institutions already buffer for exceptional circumstances by choosing high levels of confidence. A confidence level of 99.95%, for instance, translates into an expectation of once in 2000 scenarios. Such an expectation goes beyond what is feasible for most market participants to contemplate and thus this argument has some merit. The problem here is that the accuracy of the likelihood of default might be severely affected by changes in correlations, especially if return distributions are fat-tailed or skewed. The relevance of this particular issue would depend on the portfolio of the particular institution.

Appropriate risk measures: VAR *versus* Tail VAR

Economic capital modelling boils down to estimating a loss distribution and determining the buffer capital needed, given a pre-specified confidence level. This approach is tailored to equity stakeholders as this group is primarily interested in the loss-profile until the point that the firm is insolvent. A first objective of supervisors is pre-empting default, and the point of departure is thus substantively similar to that of equity-owners. In addition, however, supervisors are, as delegated monitors of policyholders and deposit holders, also interested in the distribution of losses once insolvency is triggered. They generally have to assure that in the resolution phase, after an institution is declared bankrupt, policyholders' and deposit holders' interests are properly taken care off. This will be less costly if a bankruptcy has been caused by a marginal loss (above equity) compared to a situation where almost all the assets are worthless.

To reflect supervisors' concern about extreme losses, a risk measure such as Tail VAR naturally comes to mind. This measure is the average value of losses, given that the confidence level is breached and would thus much better suit supervisors' needs. However, Tail VAR results have not yet gained the widespread acceptance VAR numbers have. This is for instance also reflected in the present supervisory approaches that have yet to adopt Tail VAR methods in any broad sense.[7] In addition, it becomes technically increasingly difficult to accurately estimate Tail VAR numbers as the confidence level is increased. This reflects the difficulty in estimating the tail of the distribution.

The systemic impact of model convergence and limited data availability

A concern that has been raised is that if institutions all use the same models, their reaction to a common shock will also become more similar. An often-cited example, especially in the aftermath of the 1987 stock market crash, was that model-based automated stop loss programmes were to blame for the severity of the market movements, although the present consensus seems to be that substantive evidence for this allegation has failed to materialise.

Moreover, supervisors' use of mechanical rules in calculating capital adequacy does in practice introduce the same model across all institutions. Especially if these mechanical rules "bite" for a significant part of the population of supervised institutions and are applied with excessive vigour this could lead to a joint reaction with systemic implications. The present move towards firm-specific internal models thus increases the diversity in models used.

However, in the survey of the state-of-play in the previous chapter we concluded that the economic capital models are substantively similar. This would indicate that institutions would indeed become more similar in their reactions to shocks, given a similar risk profile. This concern would seem to be premature as the diversity of opinion across institutions about the effects of specific shocks still builds in a buffer against herd behaviour. Two aspects can be discerned in this respect. First, economic capital modelling could lead to a shift in the composition of the activities institutions undertake and hence to a change in the exposures that institutions have on their books. This shift should be driven by the correct pricing of risks. In the short term, this might lead some or all institutions to discover previously undervalued area(s), where margins are higher. Institutions would then all like to expand their business in these profitable areas and institutions would thus become more similar. In the longer term, however, this dynamic should not necessarily lead to more similar risk profiles. Each institution could take on any exposure as long as the price charged covers the risk but these exposures do not necessarily have to be the same.

A second aspect leading to similar responses is that economic capital models are: (1) more risk sensitive, and (2) built on the same principles or by the same suppliers. Increased risk sensitivity can, especially from a prudential point of view, only been seen as an improvement. Risks that were previously present but went undetected are now being brought to the surface.

The latter issue, model convergence, could lead to supervisory concerns. The use of similar models will not so much be a problem if models are built in-house or, to a lesser extent, are truly custom-built by external suppliers. In this case, fitting the model to the characteristics of a firm is likely to introduce sufficient model variation across firms. If, however, modelling is outsourced to external parties with a significant market share who apply an off-the shelf approach, individual firms' reactions might indeed become more similar. What should then especially worry supervisors is that these models could all error in the same direction.

A variation to this argument emerges if data is scarce. Since many banks lack sufficient data to accurately estimate key parameters, especially in the early phase of implementation, external data is used. This is accepted practice in the area of credit and operational risk, for instance. These shared data could, however, be biased in some way. If this error is pervasive, the use of similar external data will lead to similar erroneous reactions of individual institutions to shared external shocks and thus financial stability in the aggregate might be strained.[8]

Partial use

Institutions generally start to model the risks that are most important in their business and are relatively easy to model. Building on these first models, other risk types that are either less important or more difficult to model are tackled. Thus although some economic capital models might not give a complete picture of all aspects of an institution's risk profile, for some parts of the risk profile there might nevertheless be valuable information in the model's result. The question emerges as to how to best use this information.

A starting point could be the overview of the reliability of modelling in the various risk types given in the previous chapter's survey of the state-of-play in economic capital models. The overview showed that on the whole the following hierarchy holds for both sectors: market, credit, insurance (if applicable), operational and business risk. Furthermore, institutions were nearly unanimous about the reliability of models on the banking side while on the insurance side views sometimes differed considerably. It is therefore conceivable that supervisors will develop methods and procedures for model acceptance in line with the discerned hierarchy. These methods and procedures will focus on the reliability of the models and whether the models genuinely improve risk management in the institution. One approach could, for instance, be to apply multiplication factors linked to the robustness of the models. Another approach has been used in the Advanced Measurement Approach for operational risk included in the Basel Framework. Here regulators have chosen to aim for a standard closer to best practice rather than industry standard. This has the advantage that the regulatory standard is quite advanced. The downside, however, is that for many institutions the operational risk management framework still needs significant development.

Definition of capital

One point that would most likely require some effort to reconcile is the definition of capital for internal and supervisory use. As noted in the introduction, the move from the traditional accounting-based approaches to capital to an economic-value-based approach will at times be strenuous. Economic capital models deliver target levels of capital to which available capital should converge. In this context, available capital instruments are those funds that have loss absorbing capacity. In the accounting-based regulatory definition of capital, the definition of capital also includes subordinated debt, under some restrictions.

Although institutions in our sample differ in what instruments economic capital amounts are intended to cover, it is clear that the industry and the regulatory definition of capital are not equal. This might in turn lead to confusion in the Supervisory Review and thus supervisors will have to be particularly attentive to this issue. One possible solution, which would warrant consistency with the first pillar, would be to require institutions to provide a reconciliation of economic capital planning in terms of regulatory capital (own funds). The most important issue here, however, is that institutions develop economic capital models that deliver accurate target capital levels.

Home-host issues in economic capital modelling

All large institutions operate in more than one jurisdiction and this raises a number of important practical issues. The most important of these are, first, the regulatory approval of the economic capital model used and, second, the allocation of diversification benefits. We will discuss these two issues in turn. Before financial conglomerates are allowed to use their economic capital models for any regulatory use, supervisors in all the relevant jurisdictions should agree that the model provides an accurate picture of all the relevant risks. This will probably give rise to a procedure very similar to the procedure for validation of credit risk models. Supervisors will exchange information among themselves and possibly the home supervisor will take the lead. Once all supervisors of significant subsidiaries agree, institutions could start using the economic capital model for supervisory purposes. Alternatively, some subset of supervisors might allow the model's use before consensus is reached. All in all, this seems like a practical issue that interested parties should be able to find a solution to.

The second important issue in home host relations is the treatment of diversification benefits. As has been discussed in previous chapters, these diversification benefits can be substantial and reflect risk reduction because (part of) the conglomerate is viewed as a whole. Once the diversification benefit has been determined and acknowledged the next step is the allocation of this benefit. In the context of our present discussion we abstract from allocative issues within jurisdictions and focus on the issues across jurisdictions. Here the diversification benefits as a result of the joint operation of two separate entities or business units will have to be allocated to one or both of these entities.

One possibility is that a host supervisor would insist on stand-alone capitalisation of a business unit in its jurisdiction. A legitimate argument for the host supervisor to require such a level of capitalisation is that in case the subsidiary runs into trouble, the necessary capital might fail to materialise in their jurisdiction because other supervisors might disallow capital transfers. The institution would in this case be forced by the host supervisor to hold more capital in its foreign subsidiary. Technically, the institution could accommodate this within its economic capital model by recalculating (parts of) the model on a stand-alone basis. A similar issue emerges within jurisdictions if institutions are legally required to hold sufficient capital on a solo basis.

If, in addition to the host supervisor's request for solo capitalisation, the home supervisor is then also led to annul the diversification benefit brought about by the foreign subsidiary, this implies that (part of) the diversification benefit would, in practice, not be acknowledged. The equally valid argument for the home supervisor would be that allowing host supervisors to insist on stand alone capitalisation and, at the same time, still recognising *all* diversification benefits would imply under-capitalisation in the home jurisdiction.

CONCLUDING REMARKS

Developments in the regulatory arena have paved the way for further consideration of economic capital models for supervisory use. Three developments stand out in particular. First, the implementation of the European Financial Conglomerates Directive. This Directive has made communication between the various supervisors with legitimate interests and financial conglomerates easier. Second, both in the banking and the insurance industry new capital adequacy frameworks are being implemented in the (relatively near) future. Both these frameworks allow the use of internal models to a certain extent. Third, the institutional structure of supervision has seen material changes in a number of countries and in many cases this has brought together banking and insurance (line-) supervision within a single organisation. Taken together, these developments have made the discussion of economic capital models feasible and fruitful.

In the chapters so far the focus has been on risk measurement and not so much on how this measurement process should be embedded within the institution. Supervisors feel that the trust an institution itself puts in any model is a good indicator of the faith that the supervisor should have in the model. A precondition is that the model has sufficient impact internally. To warrant the proper overall implementation, we have discussed the high-level principles that could guide supervisors and institutions in this respect in Section 3. Important aspects that can be stressed in this respect are that ultimate ownership of economic capital modelling should lie with the institutions, that such a model should be properly embedded in the organisation and that both supervisors and management should be attentive that assessing the validity of the models is done with sufficient care.

Even though the arguments in favour of using economic capital models are persuasive there are also a number of concerns raised, especially by supervisors. For instance, one concern discussed was that the use of economic capital models for regulatory purposes could be detrimental to competition. Another concern is that model outcomes might not be robust to levels of stress exceeding those used to design the model. Do, for instance, the assumptions about correlations still hold in times of severe market stress? Finally, the home-host aspect of this discussion was touched upon. Since financial conglomerates operate in numerous jurisdictions, many supervisors have legitimate interests in model acceptance and model use. The issue of coordination of the flow of information and the assignment of responsibility should thus (remain to) receive sufficient attention.

Notwithstanding these and other concerns, introducing economic capital models in the supervisory framework does provide a positive stimulant to improving risk awareness, measurement and management. By itself this development will not immediately solve all the imperfections in risk management we see today but given time it will certainly improve risk management.

Author of this chapter:
Iman van Lelyveld, DNB

1   See also Tiesset and Troussard (2005).
2   If the financial conglomerate is not headed by a regulated entity, the coordinator is appointed on the basis of the relative size and jurisdiction of the regulated sectors or entities within the conglomerate. If the head office is outside the EEA, the third country regulator can be "equivalent", in which case consultation is necessary, or if the regulator is not "equivalent", the EEA supervisors can force their role as coordinator.
3   Article 6.1 and 6.2 of the Financial Conglomerates Directive.
4   Technical principles 2, in Annex 1 of the Financial Conglomerates Directive.
5   See Masciandaro (2005) for an overview of theoretical considerations and an account of recent experiences.
6   See Manson and Hall (2005) for a possible outline of such a plan.
7   Except for Canadian financial regulation, where Tail VAR computations are prescribed by the OSFI for dynamic solvency capital assessments.
8   Note, however, that even with abundant data and clearly defined product characteristics pricing is not straightforward, as discussed by Walwyn and Byers (1997), for instance. In a survey by the Bank of England, market participants disagreed quite markedly on the pricing of a completely standard FX option. For a European-style Sterling/Deutschmark straddle (10-month forward option at-the-money) they found a 2.7% standard deviation in the value and even larger disagreements for the "Greeks". With more complex products disagreements naturally increases and this would increase the variability in reactions to similar shocks. A current example is the wide variation in pricing of constant maturity swaps (CMS) structures (see Sawyer 2005).

Annex A: Coherent and Insurance Risk Measures

A coherent risk measure (Artzner *et al* 1999) satisfies the following set of consistency rules:

1. *sub-additivity* –   for all random losses X and Y,
$$\rho(X + Y) \leq \rho(X) + \rho(Y)$$
2. *monotonicity* –   if $X \leq Y$ for each outcome, then
$$\rho(X) \geq \rho(Y)$$
3. *positive homogeneity* – for all positive constant b, $\rho(bX) = b\rho(X)$
4. *translation invariance* – for all constant α, $\rho(X + \alpha r) = \rho(X) - \alpha$,
with r the return of a riskless asset

Insurance risk measures represent a relaxation of the coherent risk measure, where the translation invariance property is replaced by two other properties (Jarrow 2002):

4a. *Translation monotonicity* – for all $\alpha > 0$,
$$\rho(X + \alpha r) < \rho(X) < \rho(X - \alpha r)$$
4b. *Boundary relevance* –   for all X,
with $X < 0$, X nonempty, $\rho(X) > 0$

With respect to the required properties of a coherent risk measure, the *standard deviation* risk measure does not satisfy the monotonicity property; the *lower semi-standard deviation* and *VAR* do not satisfy the sub-additivity property. The *put option premium* risk measure is not coherent, but satisfies the properties of the insurance measure. Theoretically, it has been proven that the insurance risk measure refers to the same so-called acceptance set as a

Table 9 Definitions of risk measures in use

Standard deviation	$\rho_{st}(X) = \sigma(X)$
Lower semi-standard deviation	$X^- = \begin{cases} -X, & X < 0 \\ 0, & X \geq 0 \end{cases}$
	$\rho_{semi}(X) = -E(X) + \sigma([X - E(X)]^-)$
VAR at level $\alpha \in (0, 1)$	$\rho_{VAR}(X) = -\inf\{x \mid P[(X) \leq x \cdot r] > \alpha\}$
Conditional VAR/expected shortfall/Tail VAR at level $\alpha \in (0, 1)$	$\rho_{CVAR}(X) = -E[X/r \mid X/r \leq -\rho_{VAR}(X)]$
Wang transform (Wang 2001)	$\rho_{WT}(X) = E^*(X) = \int\limits_{-\infty}^{0} g(F(x))dx + \int\limits_{0}^{\infty} [1 - g(F(x))]dx$
	with $g(u) = \Phi[\Phi^{-1}(u) - \lambda]$ and Φ the standard normal cumulative distribution function
Put option premium (Jarrow 2002)	$\rho_{PO}(X) = \dfrac{E(\max[-X, 0])}{r}$

coherent risk measure, which means that decisions are taken with the same amount of information.

The Wang transform (Wang 2001) is developed to pay attention to low-frequency and high-severity losses. For most lines of business in banking, the shape of the distribution function should not have this form, although the exposures in telecom business, for example, may represent a low-frequency/high-severity loss shape; in insurance it is a relevant item. However, in its current stage, the Wang transform is more a theoretical risk measure with nice properties, but the intuitive meaning of the risk measure is not very clear.

Thus, only the Tail VAR (Table 9, row 4) and the Wang transform (Table 9, row 5) risk measures are coherent; the put option premium risk measure satisfies the properties of the insurance risk measure. Note that, if a risk measure is coherent, it also belongs to the insurance risk measure while the other way around does not hold.

Annex B: Example of Violation of Sub-Additivity Property of the VAR Measure

Suppose, we have 100 different bonds $X(i)$, $i = 1, ..., 100$, iid distributed, with probability of default equal to 10% and a reward of US$20 of the period end coupon when it does not default. Suppose each bond has a face value of US$100. The P&L of each bond is then

$$X(i) = \begin{cases} -100 & \text{with probability } 0.10 \\ +20 & \text{with probability } 0.90 \end{cases} \quad i = 1, ..., 100$$

Consider two distinct portfolios P_j, $j = 1, 2$,

$$P_1 : X(1) + \cdots + X(100)$$
$$P_2 : 100 \times X(1)$$

Consider the following set of 10 scenarios and a VAR measure at a confidence level of 95%.

Scenario	P_1	P_2
1	800	2000
2	800	2000
3	800	2000
4	800	2000
5	800	2000
6	800	2000
7	800	2000
8	800	2000
9	800	2000
10	800	−10,000
VAR@95%	800	−10,000

It is easy to check that at a confidence interval α, the $VAR(P_1) > VAR(P_2) = 100 \times VAR(X(1))$, hence sub-additivity is not satisfied. On the basis of the VAR measure, the non-diversified portfolio is preferred, which intuitively is more risky; *diversification* of the portfolio has *increased* the measure of risk, while the "piling up" of risky bonds issued by the same company has remained undetected.

List of Abbreviations

ALAE	Allocated loss adjustment expenses
ALM	Asset and Liability Management
ANZ	Australian New Zealand Bank
BCBS	Basel Committee on Banking Supervision
BHC	Bank holding companies
CAPM	Capital asset pricing model
CEA	Comité Européen des Assurances
CEBS	Committee of European Banking Supervisors
CEIOPS	Committee of European Insurance and Occupational Pensions Supervisors
CESR	Committee of European Securities Regulators
CFM	Cash flow mismatch
CFT	Cash flow testing
CMS	Constant maturity swaps
CRD	Capital Requirements Directive
CRO-forum	Chief Risk Officer forum
DNB	De Nederlandsche Bank
EAD	Exposure at default
ECB	European Central Bank
ECOFIN	Economic and Finance Ministers of the EU
EEA	European Economic Area
ES	Expected shortfall
ERM	Enterprise-wide risk management
EVT	Extreme Value Theory
FX	Foreign exchange
FSA	Financial Services Authority
GC	Groupe Consultatif
GDP	Gross Domestic Product
IAA	International Actuarial Association
IAIS	International Association of Insurance Supervisors

IBNR	Incurred but not reported
ICAAP	Internal Capital Adequacy Assessment Process
ING	Internationale Nederlanden Group
IRB	Internal ratings based
KPMG	Klynveld Peat Marwick Goerdeler
Lamfallusy report	Report prepared by the Committee of Wise Men on the Regulation of European Securities Markets
LDA	Loss distribution approach
LGD	Loss given default
LTCM	Long Term Capital Management
OSFI	Office of the Superintendent of Financial Institutions (Canada)
P&C	Property and casualty (insurance)
PD	Probability of default
PML	Probable maximum loss
PVK	Pensioen- & Verzekeringkamer (Pension and Insurance Supervisory Authority of the Netherlands)
RAROC	Risk-adjusted return on capital
ROC	Return on capital
ROE	Return on equity
RORAC	Return on risk-adjusted capital
TCE	Tail Conditional Expectation
UBS	Union Bank of Switzerland
UCITS	Undertakings for collective investment in transferable securities
VAR	Value-at-risk
WECM	Working Group on Economic Capital Models

References

Artzner, P., 1999, "Application of Coherent Risk Measures to Capital Requirements in Insurance," *North American Actuarial Journal*, **3(2)**, pp 11–25.

Artzner, P., F. Delbaen, J.-M. Eber, and D. Heath, 1999,"Coherent Measures of Risk," *Mathematical Finance*, **9(3)**, pp 203–28.

BCBS, 2005, "International Convergence of Capital Measurement and Capital Standards: A Revised Framework" (Basel: Bank for International Settlements).

BCBS, 1996,"Overview of the Amendment to the Capital Accord to Incorporate Market Risk" (Basel: Bank for International Settlements).

Berben, R.-P. and J. Jansen, 2005,"Bond Market and Stock Market Integration in Europe." *DNB Working Paper Series, 60.*

Berg-Yuen, P. E. K. and E. A. Medova, 2004, "Economic Capital Gauged." *Working Paper Judge Institute of Management, 7.*

Berger, P. G. and E. Ofek, 1995, "Diversification's Effect on Firm Value," *Journal of Financial Economics*, **37(1)**, pp 39–65.

Bernstein, P.L., 1996, *Against the Gods: The Remarkable Story of Risk* (New York: John Wiley & Sons).

Bessis, J., 2002, *Risk Management in Banking* (Chichester: John Wiley & Sons).

Bikker, J. A., and I. P. P. Van Lelyveld, 2003,"Economic Versus Regulatory Capital for Financial Conglomerates," T. G. Kuppens,

H. M. Prast and S. A. T. Wesseling, *Banking Supervision at the Crossroads* (Cheltenham, U.K.: Edward Elgar Publishing).

Board of Governors of the Federal Reserve System, 1999, "Assessing Capital Adequacy in Relation to Risk at Large Banking Organizations and Others with Complex Risk Profiles," *Board of Governors SR letter*, pp 99–18.

Boyd, J. H. and S. L. Graham, 1988, "The Profitability and Risk Effects of Allowing Bank Holding Companies to Merge with Other Financial Firms: A Simulation Study," *Federal Reserve Bank of Minneapolis Quarterly Review*, **12(2)**, pp 3–20.

Boyd, J. H., S. L. Graham and R. S. Hewitt, 1993, "Bank Holding Company Mergers with Nonbank Financial Firms: Effects on the Risk of Failure," *Journal of Banking & Finance*, **17(1)**, pp 43–63.

Boyle, P., M. Hardy, and T. Vorst, 2005, "Life after Var," *The Journal of Derivatives*, **13(1)**, pp 48–55.

Brender, A., 2002, "The Use of Internal Models for Determining Liabilities and Capital Requirements," *North American Actuarial Journal*, **6(2)**, pp 1–10.

CEBS, 2004, "The Application of the Supervisory Review Process under Pillar 2".

Chatterjee, S., M. H. Lubatkin, and W. S. Schulze, 1999,"Towards a Strategic Theory of Risk Premium: Moving Beyond Capm," *Academy of Management Review*, **4(3)**, pp 556–67.

Clark, C. J. and S. Varma, 1999, "Strategic Risk Management: The New Competitive Edge," *Long Range Planning*, **32(4)**, pp 414–24.

Credit Suisse, 1997, "Creditrisk+".

CRO, 2005, "A Framework for Incorporating Diversification in the Solvency Assessment for Insurers".

Cumming, C. M. and B. J. Hirtle, 2001, "The Challenges of Risk Management in Diversified Financial Companies," *Federal Reserve Bank of New York, Economic Policy Review*, **7(1)**, pp 1–17.

Daníelsson, J., 2002, "The Emperor Has No Clothes: Limits to Risk Modelling," *Journal of Banking & Finance*, **26(7)**, pp 1273–96.

De Vries, C. G., G. Samorodnitsky, B. N. Jorgensen, S. Mandira, and J. Daníelsson, 2005, "Subadditivity Re-Examined: The Case for Value-at-Risk," *Financial Market Group Discussion Papers, 549*.

Dev, A., ed., 2004 *Economic Capital. A Practitioner Guide* (London: Risk Publishing).

Dierick, F., 2004,"The Supervision of Mixed Financial Services Groups in Europe," *ECB Occasional Paper, 20*.

Dimakos, X. K. and K. Aas, 2003,"Integrated Risk Modelling," *NR Report, 998*.

DNB, 2006,"Firm, Financial".

DNB, 2005, "Principles for a Financial Assessment Framework".

Dorey, M. and P. Joubert, 2005,"Modelling Dependencies: An Overview," *The Staple Inn Actuarial Society*.

Embrechts, P., A. J. McNeil, and D. Straumann, 2002, "Correlation and Dependence in Risk Management: Properties and Pitfalls," M. Dempster, *Risk Management; Value at Risk and Beyond*. (Cambridge: Cambridge University Press), pp 176–223.

Estrella, A., 2001, "Mixing and Matching: Prospective Financial Sector Mergers and Market Valuation," *Journal of Banking & Finance*, **25(12)**, pp 2367–92.

European Commission, 2005, "Directive 2005/1/Ec Establishing a New Organisational Structure for Financial Services Committees." *Official Journal, L 079, 24/3/2005 P. 0009–0017*.

Evans, M., N. Hastings, and B. Peacock, 1993, *Statistical Distributions* (New York: John Wiley & Sons).

Froot, K. A. and J. C. Stein, 1998, "Risk Management, Capital Budgeting, and Capital Structure Policy for Financial Institutions: An Integrated Approach," *Journal of Financial Economics*, **47(1)**, pp 55–82.

FSA, 2003, "The Firm Risk Assessment Framework".

Groupe Consultatif, 2005, "Diversification," *Technical Paper*, October.

Gully, B., W. Perraudin, and V. Saporta, 2001, "Capital Requirements for Combined Banking and Insurance Activities," *Banks & Systemic Risk Conference* (London: Bank of England).

Gupton, G. M., C. Finger, and M. Bhatia, 1997, "Creditmetrics: Technical Document".

Hall, C., 2002, "Economic Capital: Towards an Integrated Risk Framework," *Risk,* pp 33–6, October.

Harley, E. and S. Davies, 2001, "Low Inflation: Implications for the Fsa," *FSA Occasional Paper Series, 14.*

Holton, G.A., 2004, "Defining Risk," *Financial Analysts Journal,* **60(6),** pp 19–25.

IAA, 2002, "Report of Solvency Working Party: Prepared for Iaa Insurance Regulation Committee," *International Actuarial Association.*

IAA, 2003, "A Global Framework for Insurer Solvency Assessment, Iaa Risk-Based Capital Solvency Structure Working Party, a Draft Report."

IAIS, 2005A, "A New Framework for Insurance Supervision: Towards a Common Structure and Common Standards for the Assessment of Insurer Solvency (Framework Paper)".

IAIS, 2005B, "Towards a Common Structure and Common Standards for the Assessment of Insurer Solvency: Cornerstones for the Formulation of Regulatory Financial Requirements (Cornerstones Paper)".

Jarrow, R. A., 2002, "Put Option Premiums and Coherent Risk Measures," *Mathematical Finance,* **12(2),** pp 135–42.

Joint Forum, 2003, "Trends in Risk Integration and Aggregation" (Basel: Bank for International Settlements).

Jorion, P., 2001, *Value at Risk* (London: McGraw-Hill).

Kealhoffer, S., 1995, *Portfolio Management of Default Risk* (San Francisco: KMV Corporation).

Kiesel, R. and R. Schmidt, 2004, "A Survey of Dependency Modelling: Copulas, Tail Dependency and Estimation," W. Perraudin, *Structured Credit Products* (London: Risk Publishing).

Koyluoglu, H. U. and J. Stoker, 2002, "Honour Your Contribution." *Risk,* April, pp 90–4.

KPMG, 2002, "Study into the Methodologies to Assess the Overall Financial Position of an Insurance Undertaking from the Perspective of Prudential Regulation," KPMG.

Kuritzkes, A. and T. Schuermann, 2006,"What We Know, Don't and Can't Know About Bank Risks: A View from the Trenches," Diebold F. X. and R. Herring, *The Known, the Unknown and the Unknowable in Financial Risk Mangement* (Princeton: Princeton University Press).

Kwan, S. H. and E. S. Laderman, 1999, "On the Portfolio Effects of Financial Convergence: A Review of the Literature," *Federal Reserve Bank of San Francisco Economic Review*, **2**, pp 18–31.

Kwast, M. L., 1989, "The Impact of Underwriting and Dealing on Bank Returns and Risks." *Journal of Banking & Finance*, **13(1)**, pp 101–25.

Laderman, E. S., 2000, "The Potential Diversification and Failure Reduction Benefits of Bank Expansion into Nonbanking Activities," *Federal Reserve Bank of San Francisco, Working Paper*, 2000–01.

Lamont, O. A. and C. Polk, 2002, "Does Diversification Destroy Value? Evidence from the Industry Shocks," *Journal of Financial Economics*, **63(1)**, pp 51–77.

Lawrence, M., 2000, "Marking the Cards at Anz," *Operational Risk Suplement* (London: Risk Publishing), pp 5–8.

Lown, C. S., C. L. Osler, P. E. Strahan, and A. Sufi, 2000, "The Changing Landscape of the Financial Services Industry: What Lies Ahead?" *Federal Reserve Bank of New York Economic Policy Review*, pp 39–55.

Manson, B. and C. Hall, 2005, "Building a Capital Plan," *Risk*, pp 62–4, October.

Masciandaro, D., ed. *The Handbook of Central Banking and Financial Authorities in Europe: New Architectures in the Supervision of Financial Markets*. London: Edward Elgar Publishing, 2005.

Matten, C., 2001, *Managing Bank Capital* (Chichester: John Wiley & Sons).

McNeil, A. J., R. Frey, and P. Embrechts, 2005, *Quantitative Risk Management* (Princeton: Princeton University Press).

Merton, R., 1974, "On the Pricing of Corporate Debt: The Risk Structure of Interest Rates," *Journal of Finance*, **29**, pp 449–70.

Miller, M. H., 1998, "The Modigliani Miller Propositions after Thirty Years," J. M. Stern and D. H. J. Chew, *The Revolution in Corporate Finance*. (Malden: Blackwell Business), pp 99–110.

Modigliani, F. and M. H. Miller, 1958, "The Cost of Capital, Corporate Finance and the Theory of Investment," *American Economic Review*, **48(3)**, pp 261–97.

Myers, S. C. and N. S. Majluf, 1984, "Corporate Financing and Investment Decisions When Firms Have Information That Investors Do Not Have," *Journal of Financial Economics*, **13(2)**, pp 187–221.

Nuxoll, D. A., 1999, "Internal Risk-Management Models as a Basis for Capital Requirements." *FDIC Banking Review*, pp 18–29.

OWC, 2001, "Study on the Risk Profile and Capital Adequacy of Financial Conglomerates" (London: Oliver, Wyman & Company).

Prast, H. M. and I. P. P. Van Lelyveld, 2005, "New Architectures in the Regulation and Supervision of Financial Markets: The Netherlands," D. Masciandaro, *The Handbook of Central Banking and Financial Authorities in Europe: New Architectures in the Supervision of Financial Markets* (London: Edward Elgar Publishing), pp 311–54.

PWC, 2004,"Enterprise-Wide Risk Management for the Insurance Industry," Price Waterhouse Coopers.

Robinson, G., 2001, "The Destructive Power of 'Best Practice'." *Risk*, September, pp 123–25.

Rosenberg, J. V. and T. Schuermann, 2006 "A General Approach to Integrated Risk Management with Skewed. Fat-Tailed Distributions," *Journal of Financial Economics*, **79(3)**, pp 569–614.

Saita, F., 2004, "Risk Capital Aggregation: The Risk Manager's Perspective," *Working paper NEWFIN*.

Santomero, A. M. and E. J. Chung, 1992, *Evidence in Support of Broader Bank Powers* (New York: New York University, Salomon Center).

Santos, J. A. C., 1998, "Commercial Banks in the Securities Business: A Review," *Journal of Financial Services Research,* **14(1),** pp 35–60.

Sawyer, N., 2005, "A Difference of Opinion." *Risk,* October, pp 20–2.

Slijkerman, J. F., D. Schoenmaker, and C. G. De Vries, 2005, "Risk Diversification by European Financial Conglomerates." *Tinbergen Discussion Paper, 110.*

Societies of Actuaries, 2002, *Economic Capital Survey* (Schaumburg, Ill.: Societies of Actuaries).

Societies of Actuaries, 2004, *Speciality Guide on Economic Capital* (Schaumburg, Ill.: Societies of Actuaries).

Tiesset, M. and P. Troussard, 2005, "Regulatory Capital and Economic Capital," *Banque de France Financial Stability Review,* **7,** pp 59–74.

UK Working Party, 2003, "Risk and Capital Assessment and Supervision in Financial Firms," *Proceedings of the Finance and Investment conference 2003.*

Wall, L. D., 1987, "Has Bank Holding Companies' Diversification Affected Their Risk of Failure?," *Journal of Economics and Business,* **39(4),** pp 313–26.

Walwyn, H. and W. Byers, 1997, "The Valuation of Options," *Financial Stability Review, Bank of England,* **3,** pp 18–28.

Wang, S. S., 2001, "A Risk Measure That Goes Beyond Coherence" (Itasca, Ill.: SCOR Reinsurance Co).

Wilson, T., 1997, "Portfolio Credit Risk, Part 1." *Risk,* September, pp 111–17.

Yamai, Y. and T. Yoshiba, 2002, "Comparative Analysis of Expected Shortfall and Value-at-Risk (2): Expected Utility Maximization and Tail Risk." *Bank of Japan Monetary and Economic Studies.*

Index

A
AAA rating 158
Acceptance set 169
Accrual valuation 75
Actuarial approach, for retail
    products 39
Actuarial models 39-40
Adverse realisations 41
Allocated loss adjustment
    expenses (ALAE) 45, 173
ALM risk
    drivers of 30
    in Dutch insurance environment
    30
Artzner et al (1999) 62, 64, 169
Asia crisis (1997) 84
Asset and Liability (ALM) 173
Australian New Zealand Bank
    (ANZ) 51, 173
Average correlation values 87

B
Bank holding companies (BHC)
    104, 173
Banking institutions, on credit risk
    13
Basel Capital Adequacy
    Framework 134
Basel Committee on Banking
    Supervision (BCBS) 20,
    173
    (1996) 35
    (2001) 100
    (2005) 49, 138
Basel Standardised Approach
    121

Berg-Yuen and Medova (2004)
    105–6, 122
Berger and Ofek (1995) 104
Bernstein (1996) 16, 135
Bessis (2002) 11, 56
Bikker and Van Lelyveld (2003)
    105, 112
Bikker, J. 3
Binomial distribution 43
Book-value accounting 35
Bottom-up approach 5, 53, 126
Boughanmi, M. 3
Boyd and Graham (1988) 112
Boyd et al (1993) 104, 112
Boyle et al (2005) 77
Brender (2002) 78
Business or strategic risk
    assumptions 132
    consistency 132–3
    definition and risk drivers of
        52–5
    inclusion of risk self-assessment
        132
    information on performance
        and risk driver 132
    management action 132
    use of external data 132
    validation 133

C
CAMELS approach 21
Capital asset pricing model
    (CAPM) 173
Capital, definition of 163–4
Capital Requirements Directive
    (CRD) 21, 140, 173

Cash flow mismatch (CFM) 31–2, 173
Cash flow testing (CFT) 32, 173
Catastrophe risk 119
CEBS, release of High Level Principles 149
"Cherry-picking" 151
Chief Risk Officer Forum (CRO-forum) 117, 173
Coherent risk measures 62
Comité Européen des Assurances (CEA) 173
Committee of European Banking Supervisors (CEBS) 112, 173
Committee of European Insurance and Occupational Pensions Supervisors (CEIOPS) 21, 149, 173
Committee of European Securities Regulators (CESR) 173
Committee of European Securities Supervisors (CESR) 149
Concentration, definition of 36
Concentration risk 85
Confidence levels, effect of changing 159
Constant maturity swaps (CMS) 167, 173
Copulas
 and correlation 89
 use of 88
Correlation structure 82
Counterparty risk 35
Credit and insurance risks, modelling 8
Credit and transfer risk 34–40
Credit losses
 definition of 35
 probability distribution of 36
Credit risk
 assumptions 129
 consistency 130
 definition of 34, 99
 inclusion of risk self-assessment 129
 information on performance and risk drivers 129

management action 129
portfolio models 36
use of external data 129
validation 130
Credit Suisse (1997) 39
CRO (2005) 106
Cross-border credit risk 119
Crouhy et al (2001) 56

D
Daníelsson
 (2001) 64
 (2005) 64, 77
Data
 inconsistency of 109
 lack of 109
 quality 109
De Fermat, P. 15
De Nederlandsche Bank (DNB) 21, 173
Derivatives 35
Derivatives embedded, examples of 30
Dev (2004) 11
Developing risk-based supervision 24
Dierick (2004) 56
Diversification
 benefits 82, 164–5
 effects with financial conglomerate 5
 methods to assess effects of 86–8
 on real estate 105
Diversified VAR 27
DNB
 (2005) 24
 (2006) 56
Dow Jones index and euro interest rates 83
Duration gap analysis 31
Dutch Financial Assessment Framework 9

E
Earnings-at-risk 32
Economic capital 35
 in academic literature 91

appropriate time horizons in 72
confidence level in 69
definition of 14–15, 69
diversification effect as a
  percentage of 106
for financial institution 81
for less sophisticated
  institutions 120–1
for market risk 28
in measuring, monitoring and
  managing risks 17
as multiple of standard
  deviation 36
as quantile of distribution 36
for stake holders 76
by statistical distribution 62
use of 76
Economic capital allocation
  mechanisms, comparison of
  108
Economic capital models 138
  for capital market participants
    138
  as common denominator 60
  development and validation of
    125
  for different stakeholders 59
  with financial conglomerate
    1, 59
  implementation of 55, 118
  for institutions 138
  measures of risk 7-9
  objectives for 117–18
  overview of 1–10
  for policyholders and deposit
    holders 138
  principles for 149–56
  and risks, risk measures 61
  for supervisors 138
  supervisory view on 137
  time horizon and valuation
    principles in 59–77
  tool to measure risk 13
  valuation principle for 61
Efficiency risk 52
Embrechts et al (2002) 112
Enterprise-wide risk management
  (ERM) 173

Esscher approximation 56
Estrella (2001) 104, 112
European Central Bank (ECB) 173
European Economic Area (EEA)
  141, 173
European Financial
  Conglomerates Directive 165
European versus Asian economy
  100
Evans et al (1993) 56
Everts, H. 3
Expected loss (EL) 118
Expected shortfall (ES) 173
Expected transfer loss 39
Expense risk 52
Expost validation 125
Exposure at default (EAD) 118,
  173
Extreme event risk 43, 47
Extreme Value Theory (EVT)
  173

F
Fatter-tailed distributions 43
Financial Conglomerates Directive
  140–1
  important aspects of 142
Financial conglomerates,
  experiences of 69
Financial Services Association
  (FSA) 9, 173
Foreign exchange (FX) 173
Froot and Stein (1998) 75
FSA (2003) 56
FSA's arrow approach 21

G
Gamma/normal power
  distribution 56
Gelderman, M. 3
Glass-Steagall Act 112
Granularity 85
Gross Domestic Product (GDP)
  101, 173
Groupe Consultatif (GC) 88, 112,
  173
Gully et al (2001) 105, 112
Gupton et al (1997) 38

H
Hall (2002) 158
Historical simulation method 26, 27–8, 32
to calculate solvency capital for market risk 85
granularity in risk positions 85
Holton (2004) 56, 77
Horsmeier, H. 3

I
IAA
(2002) 49
(2003) 78
"Imperfect correlation" 87
Incurred but not reported (IBNR) 174
Insurance companies, on insurance-technical risks and ALM risk 13
Insurance, confidence levels in 123
Insurance risk
assumptions 130
calculation of 19
consistency 131
inclusion of risk self-assessment 131
information on performance and risk drivers 130
management action 130
use of external data 130–1
validation 131
Inter-risk diversification 102–3
Internal Capital Adequacy Assessment Process (ICAAP) 139, 174
Internal Ratings Based (IRB) 118, 174
International Accounting Standards Board (IASB) 174
International Actuarial Association (IAA) 24, 173
International Association of Insurance Supervisors (IAIS) 24, 173
Intra risk diversification 97–102

Investment theory, diversification on 79

J
Jarrow (2002) 77, 169
Joint Forum (2003) 112
Jones, O. 3

K
Kealhoffer (1995) 37, 56
Kiesel and Schmidt (2004) 83
Klaassen, P. 3
Knot, K. 3
Koyluoglu and Stoker (2002) 112
KPMG (2002) 24, 49
Kwan and Laderman (1999) 112
Kwast (1989) 112

L
Laderman (2000) 112
Lamfalussy approach 149
Lamont and Polk (2002) 104
Lapse risk 52
Latent variable models 38–9
Lawrence (2000) 51
Liersch, H. 3
Life insurers, capital requirements for 71–2
"Limited liability" 67
Loss distribution approach (LDA) 49, 174
advantage of 50
main characteristic of 50
Loss given default (LGD) 118, 174
Lown et al(2000) 112
LTCM (1998) 84

M
Manson and Hall (2005) 167
Market/ALM risk 25, 97, 127
assumptions 128
consistency 128
inclusion of risk self-assessment 128
information on performance and risk drivers 128
management action 127–8
use of external data 128

validation 128
Market risk
  definition and risk drivers of
    26
  measure of 26–7
Market-value accounting 35
Market value approach 33
Masciandaro (2005) 167
Matten (2001) 11, 17, 56
McKinsey Wilson (1997) 38
Mercer Oliver Wyman. *see* Oliver,
  Wyman & Co
Merton (1974) 37
Model reliability, relative ranking
  of 9, 127
Modigliani and Miller (1958) 65
Monnik, R. 3
Monotonicity property 63
Monte Carlo approach 26, 28, 118
Monte Carlo simulation 7, 32, 36
  to derive probability
    distributions 32
  portfolio returns based on 29
Morbidity risk 102
  definition and risk drivers of 44
Mortality rates
  calculating 42
  process of modelling future
    42
Mortality risk 102
  definition and risk drivers of
    41–2

N
Net present value approach 19
Netting 84
Non-life or property and casualty
  risk, definition and risk drivers
  of 45–9
Non-liquid assets and liabilities,
  value of 19
Numeric approach 88
Nuxoll (1999) 112

O
Office of the Superintendent of
  Financial Institutions (OSFI)
  71, 174

Oliver, Wyman & Co, report on
  risk profile and capital
  adequacy 1
"One-size-fits-all" assessment 80
One-year versus multi-period
  time horizon 73
Operational risk
  consistency 132
  definition and risk drivers
    49–52
  inclusion of risk self-assessment
    132
  information on performance
    and risk drivers 131
  management action 131
  models 127
  use of external data 131
OWC (2001) 11, 56, 81

P
P&C risk 102
Pascal, B. 15
Pensioen- & Verzekeringkamer
  (PVK) 174
"Perfect correlation" 87
"Piecewise" or "incremental"
  approach 25
Poisson distribution 43, 50
Policy
  and debt holders, perspective of
    66
  in life business 41
  types of 40
Portfolio concept, replicating
  33–4
Positive homogeneity property 63
Pouw, A. 3
Prast and Van Lelyveld (2005)
  149
Principal-agent problem 67
Probability of default (PD) 118,
  174
Probability of ruin 18–19
Probable maximum loss (PML)
  174
Property and casualty (P&C) 5,
  174
PWC (2004) 117, 120

Q

Qualitative approach 90

R

Regulatory capital, internal
    models in determining 9
Return on capital (ROC) 16, 174
Return on equity (ROE) 16, 174
Return on risk-adjusted capital
    (RORAC) 7, 174
Risk-adjusted return on capital
    (RAROC) 174
    for assessing and optimising
        risk adjusted returns 17
    and RORAC 15
Risk assessment 14
Risk drivers and aggregation 5–6
Risk management
    activities of financial institution
        14
    correlation in 83
Risk map, creation of 120
Risk measurement
    to assess risk profile 61
    and capital allocation, key
        concepts in 14
    as coherent 62
    definitions of 170
    developments in 16
    and economic capital 14–20
    examples of 63
    history of 15–17
    importance of 3–4
    relevance of coherent 63–4
    risk identification with 14
Risk modelling, approaches to
    5–7
Risk types
    classification of 5, 20
    general remarks about 122
Risk typology 20–5
Ruijgt, F. 3
"Run-off" approach 72

S

Santomero and Chung (1992) 112
Santos (1998) 104
Sawyer (2005) 167

Scenario analysis 33, 87, 90
Scorecard approach 49, 51
Shareholders, perspective of 65–6
Siegelaer, G. 3
Slijkerman et al (2005) 105
Slotting process 31
Societies of Actuaries
    (2002) 62
    (2004) 14, 112, 117, 122
Solvency II project 134
Stakeholders
    appropriate risk measures for
        66–9
    identification of 65–6
    payout to different 68
    risk measure for 65
Standard gap analysis 31
Statistical approach 87
Sterling/Deutschmark straddle
    167
Strategic risk 52
Stress test model 86
Structural models 37–8
Sub-additivity property 63
Supervisors
    internal models 10
    perspective of 66
    piecemeal approach 10
    range of objectives for 156
    Swiss Solvency Test 9, 71
Systematic risk 82

T

Tail Conditional Expectation
    (TCE) risk 71, 174
    variant of Tail VAR 71
Tiesset and Troussard (2005) 167
Time horizon 59, 77
    to determine economic capital
        61
Top-down approach 5, 53, 126
Trading versus life insurance 61
"Traditional" risk typology 25
Transfer or cross-border risk,
    definition and risk drivers of
        39
Transfer risk and credit risk
    40

ιon invariance property

ιid test 137

Νorking Party (2003) 117
ιiversified VAR 27
εxpected losses (ULs) 7, 40

alidation methods 124–5
Valuation principles, in economic
    capital modelling 74-75
Value-at-risk (VAR) 18, 32, 174
  as coherent 68
  components to calculate 18
  and expected shortfall,
    comparison of 72
  as measure of economic capital
    versus Tail VAR 160–1
Van Broekhoven, H. 3
Van Lelyveld, I. 3
VAR measure, violation of sub-
    additivity property of 171

VAR number, deriving economic
    capital from 28
Variance-covariance approach
    26–7, 32, 124
  main benefit of 27
Volatility risk 19, 42–3, 46

W
Wall (1987) 104
Walwyn and Byers (1997) 167
Wanders, H. 3
Wang (2001) 170
Working Group on Economic
    Capital Models (WECM) 2,
    174
Working Group's research agenda
    55

Y
Yamai and Yoshiba (2002) 77

Z
"Zero available capital" 75
Zero mid-rate 83

Transla
63
True

U
UK
Ur
U